The Forms of Things Unknown

The Forms of Things Unknown

Teaching Poetry Writing to Teens and Adults

Shelley Savren

ROWMAN & LITTLEFIELD
Lanham • Boulder • New York • London

Published by Rowman & Littlefield
A wholly owned subsidiary of The Rowman & Littlefield Publishing Group, Inc.
4501 Forbes Boulevard, Suite 200, Lanham, Maryland 20706
www.rowman.com

Unit A, Whitacre Mews, 26-34 Stannary Street, London SE11 4AB

Copyright © 2016 by Shelley Savren

All permissions regarding poems quoted in this text can be found in the back of the book.

All rights reserved. No part of this book may be reproduced in any form or by any electronic or mechanical means, including information storage and retrieval systems, without written permission from the publisher, except by a reviewer who may quote passages in a review.

British Library Cataloguing in Publication Information Available

Library of Congress Cataloging-in-Publication Data
Names: Savren, Shelley, author.
Title: The forms of things unknown : teaching poetry writing to teens and
   adults / Shelley Savren.
Description: Lanham, Maryland : Rowman & Littlefield, 2016.
Identifiers: LCCN 2016012663 | ISBN 9781475827927 (cloth : alk. paper) |
   ISBN 9781475827934 (pbk. : alk. paper)
Subjects: LCSH: Poetry—Study and teaching (Secondary)
Classification: LCC PN1101 .S36 2016 | DDC 808.1/071—dc23
LC record available at https://lccn.loc.gov/2016012663

∞™ The paper used in this publication meets the minimum requirements of American National Standard for Information Sciences—Permanence of Paper for Printed Library Materials, ANSI/NISO Z39.48-1992.

Printed in the United States of America

*In Memory of
Joyce Nower*

The poet's eye, in fine frenzy rolling,
Doth glance from heaven to earth, from earth to heaven;
And as imagination bodies forth
The forms of things unknown, the poet's pen
Turns them to shapes, and gives to airy nothing
A local habitation and a name.

—William Shakespeare
from *A Midsummer Night's Dream* Act 5 Scene 1

Contents

Foreword	xi
Preface	xiii
Acknowledgments	xv
Introduction: Teaching Students to Write Poetry	1
1 Getting Serious about Poems: Middle School and High School	15
2 Can Words Save Me? Teens with Mental Health Issues	43
3 Does Anybody Love Me? Working with Incarcerated Youth	55
Part I: Girls' Rehabilitation Facility	55
Part II: Colston Youth Center	68
4 The Urgent Landscape: Writing Poetry on College Campuses	85
5 I Remember: Cedar Community Center for Senior Citizens	103
6 Every Bird Can Sing: St. Madeline Sophie's Training Center	119
7 The Feminist Poet: Women Take Back Words	131
8 Freedom Journey: R. J. Donovan Maximum-Security Men's Prison	145
Appendix: Additional Exercise Ideas	163
Permissions	165
Resources	171
Index	173
About the Author	177

Foreword
Tim Dewar

Throughout junior and senior high I studied poetry in my English classes. I learned definitions of funny terms like "iambic" and "trochee." I acted like I understood the classroom discussions that flew around (and mostly over) my head. I was forced to write excruciatingly outlined essays on what they meant (and every "a" had to have at least a "b"). Once, in ninth grade, my teacher had us listen to and read along to the lyrics of "Eleanor Rigby." That pretty much ruined The Beatles for me.

Throughout my teenage years, I had good teachers; what I didn't have was a poet. Shelley Savren's *The Forms of Things Unknown* provides that poet for every classroom.

As she has in *Welcome to Poetryland*, her book on teaching poetry writing to younger students, Shelley Savren shares with us a magical and practical approach to teaching poetry writing to teens and adults. Shelley infuses her teaching with a sense of play based on a deep knowledge of poetry and students. This book is filled with poems from published and former students that today's students can relate to. All of these are surrounded by lessons and guidance for teachers and writers of all types and dispositions.

Her lessons are not tricks. Rather, they build on Shelley's attentive reading of great canonical and contemporary poets. Her readings of the professional samples show the attention of a poet. She notes the images and sounds that less experienced poets can imitate, then builds a delicate scaffold for students. The student samples published throughout the book demonstrate the power of her approach.

A teacher who follows Shelley's lead will not only teach the students how to write poetry, but also about poetry. In these pages are numerous examples that teach the terminology of poetry study. Need to teach symbolism? Let's talk about shadows. How about persona? She has that covered, too. I can't imagine any learning objective about poetry that is not addressed. I can, however, imagine crafting a unit to study poetry out of the lessons here. The challenge would be to keep it from taking over a whole year!

This book's organization lends itself to another use: Supplementing thematic units. The emphasis on writing, not just studying, poetry means that students can use writing to deepen, clarify, and communicate their thinking about the serious issues of identity, love, family, power, and the like that the study of literature addresses. I can't wait to pair some of the lessons in chapter two on identity with students' reading of *Catcher in the Rye*. No more boring essays about Holden, but poems that show who he is.

Shelley Savren's book empowers teachers and students to write poetry. In the process they will learn about poetry, themselves, and the world. I think that is what my ninth grade teacher was trying to do so long ago with a 45 rpm record. She would have had more success had she had this book.

Tim Dewar
Director of the South Coast Writing Project, an Affiliated Site
of the California and National Writing Projects

Preface

About a month after I completed a ten-session poetry-writing workshop at a high school Advanced Placement (AP) class, the teacher sent me a disk with poems that two of her students had recorded. Their poems had been accepted in a California Poets in the Schools (CPITS) statewide poetry anthology, and both teacher and students were proudly promoting them school-wide.

Just a few years earlier, I had concluded two six-month poetry-writing workshops at a maximum-security men's prison and received a letter from an inmate saying, "As a teacher, you unlocked the creativity within our hearts, something not easily done among men who have become like stone walls for fear of looking weak." Then recently, I received an email from a former college student who is now pursuing a MFA in poetry writing. She said, "I wanted to thank you for bringing poetry into my world and pushing me to write it. I have had a handful of wonderful professors . . ., but you were the first to ever make me realize that I could do something with my poetry and my words. Thank you ceaselessly for that."

This is why I teach poetry writing. The very first time I stepped into a classroom, in 1976, I had no idea how to do this. I just knew that writing poetry could change a person and it could change the world. But once I began that first workshop, I knew that I would dedicate my life to teaching poetry to anyone who would sit down with me for fifteen minutes with a pen.

The first workshops I taught were in public and alternative schools, and I saw how writing poetry was making a difference in the lives of their students; yet I wanted to reach a broader audience. I wanted to teach the "unteachables"—the outcasts of society, people who were either marginalized, in trouble, or victims of life circumstances.

Mainly, the groups I envisioned myself working with were at-risk youth in juvenile halls or in schools for teens with mental health issues, adults who were developmentally disabled, seniors in general, and women of all ages—most of whom were desperately trying to change their lives. Then the opportunity arose for me to work with men who were incarcerated, who'd made a mess of their lives and needed to reach inside and find words to express their pain or difficulties.

I also wanted to continue my work in middle schools and high schools, where students are often the most challenging to reach, and in colleges, where poetry writing could be a path that led to many doors—personal or career-oriented. It didn't matter. There was work to do, and I was and still am committed to doing it everywhere.

This book is a continuation of my previous one, *Welcome to Poetryland: Teaching Poetry Writing to Young Children*. The structure is identical, each chapter beginning with a memoir that records my experiences of conducting poetry-writing workshops for over twenty-five thousand students spanning forty years. My intention in telling these stories is also the same—to show the authenticity of each experience.

Each chapter then shifts to writing exercises, complete with introductions about poetic concepts, model poems by professionals and student poets, and open-ended writing assignments. My main purpose for writing this book is for teachers and other visiting poets to get excited about using the poetry-writing exercises in classrooms.

Students who have participated in these poetry-writing workshops over the years have become our future poets and audience members. They have taken risks to write about their lives and become vulnerable before their peers. They have stepped into the path of poetry, which affects people when they least expect it. There is always an occasion to write a poem. The way I see it, poetry transforms lives, so why not teach it to everyone?

Acknowledgments

I am fortunate to have had opportunities to teach poetry to over twenty-five thousand students over the past forty years. In 1975, California Poets in the Schools (CPITS) contacted me to conduct a poetry-writing workshop at a high school. I never applied to teach in the program, and I had no mentor, no training, and no guidance. I knew very little about teaching poetry writing and had to find my way.

Not long after that, CPITS developed a training program, but I was just thrown into a classroom and told, "Go!" Over the years, though, I have found support and guidance from other poets who teach, specifically through the CPITS program, and I have trained dozens of poets to work in schools and the community.

My first full-time poetry-teaching job began in September 1977. I was hired by the Intercultural Council of the Arts (Community Arts) of San Diego to conduct poetry-writing workshops at locations that historically had underserved populations. The project was funded by the Comprehensive Employment and Training Act (CETA). I spent a year working two to four hours a week at St. Madeline Sophie's Training Center for the Retarded, the Cedar Community Center for Seniors, and the Sierra Vista High School Girls' Rehabilitation Facility (GRF) for incarcerated girls in grades eight through twelve.

My biggest funding source was the California Arts Council (CAC), to which I am eternally grateful for awarding me *nine* Artist-in-Residence grants. The first three CAC grants (1978–1982) were at the Center for Women's Studies and Services (CWSS), where I conducted poetry-writing workshops and organized poetry events. The grant also allowed me to continue the workshops at GRF.

At CWSS, I met Joyce Nower, who taught me everything I know about organizing. She was a co-founder of CWSS (originally a women's studies program, the first in the nation, at San Diego State University), the Feminist Poetry and Graphics Center, Community Arts, and Exploring Family School, an alternative school. I taught poetry writing at all of those places. Without Joyce's mentorship and support, I might not have had the confidence to pursue a career in teaching poetry.

Shortly after the CAC grants at CWSS ended, I received funding three years in a row from the Combined Arts and Education Council of San Diego County (COMBO) through its National Endowment for the Arts (NEA) re-granting program. Matching funds were provided by the San Diego Office of Education Court and Community Schools Program. This funding also allowed me to keep the program alive at GRF.

Then in 1989, I was hired by ARTSREACH, a statewide program employing artists to conduct workshops in prisons. ARTSREACH was funded by UCLA and CAC as a part of its Arts-in-Corrections program. For six months, I taught workshops at the R. J. Donovan Correctional Facility, a maximum-security men's prison two miles from the Mexican border.

Meanwhile, schools throughout San Diego County at all grade levels consistently hired me to conduct poetry-writing workshops through CPITS. About two dozen school districts participated. Poway High School had a full-day writing symposium, where they brought in writers from different genres. I was hired to conduct workshops all day long. Those were amazing days for students to become immersed in writing.

When I moved to Ventura, California, in 1992, I began teaching at Oxnard Community College full-time, and soon my teaching load included creative writing. But I also continued to conduct poetry-writing workshops in the community and in schools at all grade levels throughout Ventura County—which I have always been committed to doing, even though it was on a much smaller scale than before.

In fact, soon after I arrived in Ventura County, the City of Ventura Office of Cultural Affairs funded my workshops for five years, in conjunction with the Ventura County Office of Education and CPITS, at the Frank A. Colston Youth Center, a lockdown facility. Though it was co-ed, the vast majority of those incarcerated were boys.

For the past twenty years, the City of Ventura Office of Cultural Affairs has granted funds to CPITS to conduct poetry-writing workshops specifically in the city's schools and, again, at all grade levels. I've taught in dozens of classrooms through those grants. The City of Ventura also awarded me five fellowships just to write poetry, for which I am humbly grateful.

Over the years, I have taught in thousands of classrooms in San Diego, Orange, Imperial, Los Angeles, and Ventura counties with funding from a wide variety of sources. Many schools used Gifted and Talented Education (GATE) funds, Title I money for disadvantaged students, and Special Education funds. I am also grateful to several newspapers and magazines, including *The San Diego Union-Tribune, The Los Angeles Times, The San Diego Magazine,* and *The Ventura County Star* for feature articles that promoted my programs.

The system has trusted me. Administrators have trusted me. Teachers have trusted me. Alan Murray, the principal of Phoenix School in Ventura County, hired me for three years to conduct poetry-writing workshops once a week at a lockdown facility for teens with mental health disabilities.

Many English teachers, convinced that poetry writing was the best language arts lesson for their students' writing, have contacted me year after year to teach it in their classrooms. I returned for three years to Oxnard High School in Ventura County, California, to teach students in Bonnie Horn's AP classroom. In addition, I've conducted dozens of in-service workshops for middle and high school English teachers on teaching poetry writing to their students and facilitated workshops at the CPITS annual symposiums.

I have never had a hard time convincing educators or administrators that teaching poetry writing works. Deep down, everyone wants to express himself or herself. Poetry writing also works for my students because my excitement for poetry is contagious. Teachers have easily caught this excitement, too, and I am thankful for their partnership in bringing poetry into the lives of their students.

My students have given me so much to write about. They have trusted me and have written with me. I am always seeking more experiences where I can learn what students have to teach me. In the end, it is the students to whom I owe a debt of gratitude. I thank them. I thank everyone who has supported my poetry-writing workshops along the way.

MY GRATITUDE

Once there was a little girl who dreamed about teaching poetry to everyone she met. She grew up, and her dream came true. My thanks go to all of the following people and entities:

- Oxnard College and Ventura County Community College District for granting me a sabbatical to write this book
- CAC for so many years of financial support
- all the teachers who have welcomed me into their classrooms
- all the CPITS poets who share my work and vision

- fellow poet Bruce Weigl for his support throughout the process of moving this book toward publication
- fellow poets Richard Newsham, Michelle Bitting, Vernard Maxam, and Elijah Imlay for encouragement and critical feedback on this book
- David Magallanes, Richard Newsham, and Elijah Imlay for many hours of copyediting and proofreading
- Joyce Nower for her belief in me as a poetry teacher
- COMBO of San Diego, Ventura Arts Council, the City of Ventura Office of Cultural Affairs, Community Arts, ARTSREACH, and all the other numerous funding sources that kept my workshops going over the years
- Alan Murray and so many other principals who funded my programs
- thousands of students, young and old, for trusting my guidance and taking a journey with me

May poetry fill your hearts forever and ever!

Introduction
Teaching Students to Write Poetry

Anyone who uses language can write poetry. It's important to begin all workshops with this premise and to dismiss the notion that poetry exists somewhere outside of one's self.

The whole idea behind writing poetry is not to shut out those noises which are disturbing and distracting, but rather to become immersed in the surrounding elements, to open up all five senses and take in all that is there—to swim in it, swallow it, digest it thoroughly, and then go beyond that sensory data to the warehouse of experiences that students can draw upon. If students sit with a memory or an experience, they can discover the emotion inside it and create images from there. This is the moment when a poem is conceived; this is the place where the muse dwells.

Magic Must Occur

Teaching teens and adults to write poetry entails a great deal more than merely teaching technique. Some kind of magic also has to occur. Students need to be given the freedom to explore, to break down boundaries, to create worlds. They need permission to break the rules—not just of grammar, but of linear thinking—and to make connections outside of the logical realm, which is what metaphor usually does.

Poetry, like all art, is self-expressive. It's easy. Everyone has thoughts, feelings, and ideas. Students just need permission to speak from their hearts and minds and to write. Poems are born out of an opening up, and students need to be encouraged to write about their lives and to be daring. The visiting poet or teacher provides contexts; the students create content. The visiting poet or teacher shows them colors; the students paint pictures with words.

If they learn that there is poetry in everything, they only need to find it and speak it in whatever way they choose. It doesn't matter who the students are, where they come from, or how old they are. The goal is to turn everyone on to poetry, because poetry enhances the human spirit. It heals the heart, and it also heals the world.

THE CLASSROOM TEACHER'S ROLE

When a visiting poet is conducting the workshop, before she or he comes to a classroom, many teachers have already gotten their students excited about poetry. This helps tremendously. Middle and high school teachers have been assigning poems for their students to read and sometimes analyze. In this way, the visiting poet and teacher form a partnership, spreading the excitement of poetry.

It's important for teachers to have the students buy notebooks that they can use just for poetry or to have composition books for them to write in, which the visiting poet collects at the end of the workshop, reads, and returns. In middle school and high school classes, students can often type up their drafts on classroom computers or at home and then submit them in folders. College students are usually required to submit poems in portfolios. In workshops held at community settings, the workshop leader can decide whether or not to collect the poems; however, it's useful for the students to get feedback.

In school settings, teachers are encouraged to write with the students and become a part of the community of writers. When teachers become engaged in the same writing activity as the students, it contributes to the magic. This also applies when there is no visiting poet coming to the classroom, and the teacher is conducting the workshop.

Be Spontaneous

Most teaching of poetry writing is spontaneous. The visiting poet or teacher can incorporate whatever he or she sees in the classroom into the lesson. For example, one middle school classroom had a world map on the back wall. The students discussed what life might be like in different countries. The customs, languages, and even the weather could be very different from what they experience. Since the very first lesson focused on portraying people who were different from them, the students were encouraged to use some of those observations in their poems.

When students read their poems, if they happen to use a poetic concept that hasn't yet been introduced, the visiting poet or teacher can get excited and teach that technique on the spot. For example, if someone uses personification, just write that word on the board or document camera and guess what? Not only is that student glowing, but the next week many student poems have personification in them.

HOW TO READ THROUGH THESE CHAPTERS

This book is arranged by grade level and focus population. Each chapter begins with a quote from a student and an original poem by the author of this book. This is followed by a true story about working in that particular environment with that specific population. Then exercises with model poems are presented, ready for teachers to put to use, along with student poems inspired by the exercises that can also be read as model poems. Most of the lessons can be adapted for students at any age or grade level.

THE FIRST DAY OF THE WORKSHOP

The first time the visiting poet enters a classroom, she or he smiles and offers a great big "hi." This relaxes the students. The visiting poet is always animated, so the room fills with excitement. Students can call the visiting poet by his or her first name,to create a more intimate environment.

Whether it's the visiting poet or the teacher conducting the workshop, always begin by talking about what poetry is and search for an extensive definition. Some students may say that poems are made out of "rhyming" words, and sometimes that's true. Up until the past century, almost all poems rhymed. But today, most poems are written in free verse. Explain that free verse poems don't usually rhyme or have a set pattern and that they will be writing mostly in free verse, so their poems won't rhyme.

Then list the elements that comprise a poem, including the use of imagination, the five senses, detail, color, imagery, emotion, rhythm, form, and figurative language (metaphor/simile, symbolism, and personification).

How Poems Are Like and *Not* Like Prose

No matter what grade level you are teaching, talk about how poems are like prose because they tell about something. But poems look different because all the lines don't go to the end of the page. The line lengths vary. Hold up a prose page from an essay and walk around the room with it. Then do the same with a page of poetry.

Explain that most prose, including short stories, are often longer than poems because they expand and explain more. But a poem moves faster, and the reader really needs to pay attention or else she or he will not capture its essence. Also, prose is written in indented paragraphs, while poems are written in stanzas. When poets get a new idea, they don't indent; they skip a space.

Emphasize that poetry, in contrast to prose, also uses an economy of words. Therefore, each word has to be carefully chosen to convey meaning and language must be tightened, which might mean breaking the rules of grammar and not always having complete sentences. It's important that students *know* these grammar rules, though, in order to break them. Suggest to students that they end each line with a strong noun or verb. Also establish that poetry has a kinship with music that is based on its cadence, which is often determined by reading the poem aloud.

WHAT POEMS EXPRESS AND WHERE IDEAS COME FROM

Ask, "What does a poem express?" The answer is "feelings," of course. Tell the students that they also use their five senses when they write poems. Then ask, "How is a poem like music?" The answer is that they both have a beat or rhythm. Just touch on these concepts during the first lesson and then elaborate on them with each new lesson. Ask if there's anything that they can't write about in a poem. The answer is no.

Then ask, "But where do all of these ideas come from?" Students might suggest books they read, places they visit, TV shows they watch, friends they hang out with, family they spend time with, and so on. Some say the ideas come from their feelings, and that's true. But the word you're looking for is "imagination." It will lead to the first lesson.

THE PROCESS

There is really no mystery to the process of writing poetry. Reading and writing poetry can be fun if students can relate to the poems and are encouraged to write from their own experiences. Deep down, we all want to express ourselves. And often poetry is the best way to do that. Poetry writing works when a visiting poet or teacher is excited about it. That excitement is contagious.

The process is pretty simple. First, introduce a poetic element and give an open-ended writing assignment that draws on the students' own life experiences or observations. This takes about fifteen minutes. Always read model poems by both published poets and by students their own age to bridge the gap between professionals and students and show the class that anyone can write a poem.

Also, try to choose some poems by poets from their own culture. Culture doesn't only mean race, religion, or national origin. The word is much bigger. For example, inside a prison there is a culture; in fact, there can be several cultures divided by race, crime, and so forth. The visiting poet or teacher is an outsider to that culture but has been given permission to enter in and sit on the edge—directing, observing, and hoping for success.

Question Time and Quiet Time

Once students have been given the open-ended assignment, ask if there are any questions. After questions are answered, ask who understands the assignment. Several students might raise their hands. Choose one student to repeat the assignment and then clarify anything necessary.

It's a good idea to instruct students not to talk when they write. Some people need quiet, so others need to respect that. If it's a noisy class, one technique to use is to tell them that they have two minutes to talk about their poems. Then turn out the lights and say, "On your marks, get set, *write!*" Then turn the lights back on. It works every time. The students quiet down and begin to write.

Time to Write

Have the students write in their poetry journals (or sheets of paper that will go into a poetry folder) for about fifteen to twenty minutes. If the setting is outside the classroom and/or involves adults, writing time can go as long as thirty to forty-five minutes.

Sometimes there are students who don't want to write or don't know what to write about. They usually just need encouragement. Sit next to them and talk with them about ideas for poems. Ask them questions. Sometimes you can just suggest a title or a first line, and they're off. Or if they don't like the assignment, which rarely happens, they can write about anything they want.

When they begin, circulate and assist students when necessary. Once everyone is entrenched in the process, write with the class. But keep an eye out for students who finish early and tell them that if they think they're done with their poem, to look it over to see if they can add more or give it a title, if they haven't already done so.

Forget Grammar and Spelling for Now

Remind students that these are drafts, so they don't need to worry about spelling or grammar. Taking time to look up words might interrupt the flow of thought for the poem. They can always correct spelling or revise their poem when they're done with their draft. Also, encourage nonnative speakers of English to write in their native language or to write in English and use words from their native language in their poems. Using two languages can make the poem more interesting and might make it easier for some students to keep the writing flowing.

Time to Read/Share Their Poems

The last fifteen or twenty minutes of the workshop is spent reading and responding to the poems. It's essential to create a safe environment for building trust. Trust means that no one laughs at a poem unless it's meant to be funny, and while they can write whatever they want without censoring themselves, no one reads a poem that will hurt or embarrass another classmate. These are called "safety rules."

Another "rule" is not to allow students to apologize for their poem. Tell them that everyone knows the poem is a draft and will be improved later on. They should also be discouraged from explaining too much of the poem. The best thing for them to do is just read it, *listen* to their own poem as they read it, and then allow others to respond.

Classmates should not say that they don't like something in the poem or that there is something wrong with it (especially since there's no right or wrong when writing poetry). Also, if students are reading too softly, suggest that they pretend they are on a stage and need to project their voices for the audience to hear them. Tell all students in the audience that some people have soft voices. Audience members who can't hear a poem can just sit quietly and respectfully and don't have to respond.

Offering Support

Sometimes you can offer to read the poem with a student if she or he is too shy to come up to the front of the classroom and read. Or the student can just read the poem with you from her or his seat. Begin by reading the first line. The student reads the next line and then usually forgets that someone is reading with him or her and just continues on. Students can also read their poems to partners or in small groups if there are not many reading volunteers.

Sometimes a student will cry when reading a poem, and the best thing to do is just offer support. Other students sit up and really listen, and you can tell them to be that person's friend in the hallway or wherever else they might meet. Sometimes you will have to finish reading the poem, or if the student doesn't want anyone to read the rest of the poem, that's okay, too. The key thing is to make every student feel important and that her or his poem is worthy of validation. Everyone claps after someone reads a poem.

The Yardstick of Success

Although almost everyone will write a poem, no one should be forced to write or to read, for that matter. Not everyone will want to share a poem every time, and that's always fine. The important thing is to continue to encourage students to write, to suggest ideas if necessary, and to remind them that they have imaginations full of ideas for poems.

If students are participating, then the workshop is successful. But success is an ambiguous word. Who carries the yardstick to measure it? Success can mean a developmentally disabled adult draws a circle and writes a few letters. It can be a seventh grader reading her or his poem for the first time or high school students critiquing each other's work in a supportive environment.

CURRICULUM AND LESSON PLANS

Even though it's important to teach spontaneously, there should always be a lesson plan; in fact, these chapters present a curriculum at all levels that covers various aspects of poetics and uses the four modalities—listening, speaking, reading, and writing—for different grade levels and situations. Poetry writing should be integrated across the curriculum, throughout the year, not just as a poetry unit in June.

One selling point for doing poetry-writing workshops is that they cover many aspects of language arts, and when students write poetry, their writing skills improve in other areas as well. Also, any subject can be taught through poetry. There are poems that describe social problems, historical events, and environmental catastrophes. If you happen to teach multiple subjects, like English and history, and you're teaching the Civil War, you can bring in Walt Whitman.

Or if you happen to teach science, when you're in a lab reviewing scientific method, you can show how people come up with a hypothesis by using their imaginations just as they do when they write poems. The list goes on. Also, revising poems engages mathematical and critical-thinking skills.

Following is an overview of the basic poetry-writing curriculum covered in this book.

Imagination—Poetry's First Element

The number of lessons determines how much of the poetry curriculum can be covered. But it's best to talk about the imagination as the first element of poetry. Everyone uses his or her imagination to create poems; ideas come to the imagination from everything a person does, and creativity begins there.

Everyone imagines before she or he makes choices, like imagining what an ice cream flavor will taste like before it's ordered and is handed over in a cone or what clothes to wear on a hot or rainy day, and anyone can go back into her or his memories and imagine the details of what happened in the past.

A poem can recreate a real experience, expand on it, or turn it into something new. Visionaries, scientists, and artists draw from both inspiration and imagination. The imagination is a tool for discovering worlds. It holds a warehouse of ideas that are just waiting to be discovered. It not only helps people invent and create, but it also helps them survive; it gives them hope and belief in possibilities.

Perception—The Five Senses

The next poetic concept in the curriculum presented in these chapters is often perception, that is, the use of the five senses. Putting the five senses into poems makes them come alive and seem real, so other people can relate to them. The five senses are important in life, and it's the student's job to pay attention to what she or he experiences with the five senses every day. A great example of using the senses is in Mary Oliver's poem, "Wild Geese," where she writes, "the sun and the clear pebbles of the rain/are moving across the landscapes." The reader can see, hear, and feel the rain.

Details

Another important poetic concept is the use of details in poems. Ask students to look around the room and notice a detail that they never noticed before, something that has been there for the whole year, like a crack in the ceiling or a stain on the rug. They can notice details found on bulletin boards or walls that might display posters or student writing and artwork.

Explain that poems need rich descriptions, so the reader can imagine the scene and the feeling. When writing a poem, the less vague or abstract and the more concise and specific the poem is, the more interesting it will be. Details help the reader go inside the poem, sit down, and find her or his way around; details help people relate to the poem. Tell students, "Don't write about nature; write about a tree. Better yet, write about an oak tree, an olive tree, or a palm tree in the backyard or on the street."

Color

Then there's the concept of color used in poems. Ask, "What would a black-and-white world be like? What if we could only watch black and white TV, like people had to do in the past?" Everyone agrees it would be boring. Tell students that no one wants her or his poems to be in just black and white either, unless the person is writing about shadows or darkness. An example of using color is in W. S. Merwin's poem, "How We Are Spared," when he writes, "before dawn an orange light returns to the mountains."

Feelings/Emotions

One of the most vital poetic concepts is the expression of feelings. Such expression is the heart of a poem; it's what makes poems important to write and inspiring to read. The best way to put emotions into a poem is to re-create an experience and not just state a feeling. The goal is to get readers to enter the poem and exit feeling moved in some way, to react. But the poem shouldn't tell the reader *how* to feel. Tell students, "Don't say you're 'sad'; instead, describe what happened that made you sad," like Pablo Neruda writes in his poem, "Winter Garden": "I stood on the balcony dark with mourning."

To effectively express a feeling in a poem, a poet has to go beneath the surface of the words and embed feelings in between the lines; he or she has to make a situation personal. The more specifically the poet describes what happened to make him or her feel a certain way, the stronger the poem will be. The poet will feel the emotion, and the reader will be able to experience what the poet or speaker is feeling and might relate the emotion to his or her own experiences. That's what makes poetry universal.

Imagery

Imagery is also essential in poetry because it distinguishes it from other types of writing. Ask, "What is an image? What do you get when you press a button on a camera or turn on a TV?" The answer is "a picture." Ask, "If an image is something a person can see, then what would an image be in poetry?" It's a picture made out of words, because a poet's tool is words.

Imagery is the language of poetry; it's an unusual language, a higher order of language that poets use to say something ordinary, yet different from everyday speech. Poets use their imaginations to create pictures in the readers' minds, and the language is often exquisite.

Walk up to someone in the class and tell her or him to imagine walking outside when it starts to get dark. Say, "It's getting dark. Let's go inside." Then walk up to another student and tell him or her to imagine walking outside when it starts to get dark. Say, "Night is a dark visitor." But no one talks like that. A person doesn't say, "Hey, man, night's a dark visitor." Everyone will laugh at this.

Then ask, "Which is ordinary language, and which is the language of poetry?" Everyone will agree that "night is a dark visitor" is much more interesting language and preferable for poetry. It gives the reader a picture, whatever that might be for each person. That's what images do.

Similes and Metaphors

One way to instantly create images is to use figurative language, like similes, another poetic concept presented in this book. Tell students that similes are used in poetry to compare one thing to another thing that no one would ordinarily compare it to, and the comparison might not even make sense. And when poets are comparing, they use the word "like" or "as."

First, they think of an object, then a word to describe it, and then a word to compare it to. Give as examples "The summer was *as* yellow *as* a field of daisies" or, like Yehuda Amichai writes in "Songs for a Woman," "Your body is white like sand." Emphasize the words "as" and "like."

Also, introduce metaphors and explain that they do the same comparing but without using the words "like" or "as." The thing they are comparing *becomes* the thing they're comparing it to. So the above examples would become "The summer *was* a yellow field of daisies" and "Your body *is* white sand."

Persona and Personification

Another poetic technique is the use of a persona. When someone writes in a persona, she or he uses the word "I" but pretends to be someone else, presenting that person's point of view. The poet feels what that person feels, experiences what that person experiences, and sees the world from his or her perspective. The poet basically walks in that person's shoes. This is one reason why readers can never assume that the speaker in the poem is the author. Another reason is that when poets write about their own experiences, they frequently embellish them in their poems.

Poets also use personification, giving human characteristics to something that isn't human. For example, in her poem, "The Breathing," poet Denise Levertov writes, "Trees stand/up to their knees in/fog. . . ." Point out that trees don't have knees like humans do, but from those lines, the reader can visualize a low fog on the ground.

Rhythm and Alliteration

Two of the last poetic concepts in the curriculum are rhythm and alliteration. Tell students that poems are like music because both have a "beat" or "rhythm." Ask if they can dance to a poem. The answer, of course, is yes.

Talk about different ways to put rhythm into poems. One way is to use very short, staccato lines or very long lines. Sometimes this is done by creating lists. Another way is to create syllabic patterns or repeat lines or words, as Derek Walcott does in his poem "Love After Love," where he writes, "Give wine. Give Bread. Give back your heart." Explain that traditional poetry, written before the twentieth century, had predictable patterns called meter. A certain pattern was established and continued to repeat. But in free verse, patterns are not predictable.

Then look around the room and notice patterns, for example, stripes on the American flag or plaid designs on people's clothing. Notice what's predictable and what's not. Talk about patterns in nature, like the stripes on a zebra. No two zebras have the same stripes, and no one can predict the pattern, but like patterns in free verse, everyone knows that more stripes will appear. Point out that there are patterns everywhere a person goes and that everyone has certain rhythms in his or her life, like brushing teeth every morning.

As for alliteration, just encourage students to repeat consonant sounds, for example, "the pit of the passing peach," also from Pablo Neruda's "Winter Garden." Many students use alliteration naturally, and it's a good idea to point out when they do and show how it adds music to the poem.

Form

Finally, there is form. Point out how poems look different on the page from prose. Teach students how to scan a poem for natural breath lines by reading the poem out loud and drawing slashes whenever they take a breath. Then they can recopy the poem, starting a new line at every slash and then omitting the slashes. Tell them that this is part of editing their poems, just like correcting spelling, omitting useless words, and adding more details.

FEEDBACK

One important thing to know is that if students are made to feel good about their writing, they'll want to keep writing. So feedback is important and is also tricky. It doesn't matter who you are working with. Always focus on what's working. Everyone's ego can be fragile. Many students have trouble separating their poems from themselves, and whether they act tough or not, they can get hurt by what they interpret as criticism.

Yet critiquing is a vital part of the process. It's also a form of validation. Students need to hear that someone in the class, besides the teacher or visiting poet, liked something about their poem and could relate to it.

Students Giving Feedback

When teens or adults are responding to initial drafts, simply ask one person to positively point out a detail or line that he or she liked—the more specific, the better—and then add a positive comment yourself. This form of validation encourages students to continue doing whatever others liked. For example, if you say you like the rhythm in the last two lines of the poem, that student will continue to write poems with good rhythm. The same applies to images, details, and so forth.

If the workshop is longer than eight weeks or is at an adult or college level, you can do more extensive revision with the students. Tell them that it's best to react as an audience, stating what they observed, what they think is working great in the poem, what confuses them, and what they would like to see changed.

REVISION

Always encourage students to revise their poems when they think they're done with their drafts. Of course, not all students choose to do this, and it's important to make sure that they know that there's nothing wrong with their poems as they are.

Actually, in some of the following chapters there are two sets of guidelines—one for secondary school and one for college—to use when doing revision as a whole class, and both can also be adapted for adult community settings. While the main goal is to introduce students to different aspects of poetry and get them writing, revision is an important part of the process. This is the craft part.

Embracing Craft

Craft is both hard work and ecstasy. If a student loves to write poetry, she or he will want to learn more and discover the mechanics of writing. This happens at all levels. It's the yearning that makes the student want to speak, to eventually embrace the art form and find success in writing poetry.

Every poet deals with craft differently. Explain to students that there's no right way to revise a poem. Stress that they need to read the poem aloud to hear it, in order to know if the music is working and if the poem is saying what they want it to say. Suggest that they use natural breath lines or intuit line breaks. Caution them against using abstractions, and encourage them to use specific, concrete details. In the end, the student writing the poem is in charge of deciding what to change or not change.

High school and college students, especially, need to know that serious poets embrace craft, and that means they have to read and study poetry. It's not enough to just write it. There's a lot of great poetry being published; so encourage students to read that instead of trendy rhyming poems that anyone can post online and that don't serve as good models for literature.

Students need to understand that successful poetry can be simple but it must have depth and meaning. Teachers and visiting poets can suggest book titles and encourage students to visit the contemporary poetry section in their local libraries and bookstores.

FOLLOW-UP PROJECTS

There are several follow-up projects that you can do after students complete their poems. You can have classroom poetry readings and/or readings in the community, for example, at libraries, bookstores, galleries, or coffeehouses. Nowadays, students can put their poems in blogs and post them on social media platforms, such as Facebook, Instagram, Twitter, and Tumblr. They can also put up their readings on YouTube.

Teachers can also compile class anthologies. Students type their poems on computers in their classrooms or at home and save and/or print them for anthologies. That way, they participate in another process—a publishing process, where they have control of their work and can more easily make revisions.

When making anthologies, every student should choose her or his favorite poem, revise it, and then type it in a font that's easy to read. Instruct students not to center their poems, but to type them flush left. This can be done in class or at home. Then each student contributes a poem to the anthology. The class decides on a title. Select one student to design the cover, which can be made of construction paper or thicker bond. The anthologies are then printed and can be either stapled or spiral-bound. Every student gets a copy, and one goes to the school library.

An alternative to print, of course, is an online class anthology. Teachers can easily upload student poems and compile them into an online publication, or students can be assigned to do the job. Anthologies can also be done online at no cost for workshops held in community settings. If they're printed, the workshop leader will most likely be responsible for the cost; however, sometimes there is funding available from local arts councils or other community organizations for this type of project.

Another way for students to experience the process of being a poet is by attending poetry readings, some of which are scheduled regularly in community locations. Often these readings have open mics, where anyone can get up and read a poem. Encourage students to do this for the experience and, perhaps, for extra credit. This is just one more way to make students proud of their poems.

THE ULTIMATE GOAL

When teaching poetry writing, always wear the "poetry hat." Dance on the table. Teach them the magic. Always fill the room with passion and get students excited about poetry. Transform the classroom into another world where anything can happen. Students can go on guided fantasies or take a freedom journey. They can all have a truly liberating experience. Even the toughest person can find openings for expression.

The goal is to teach students how to reach into their pockets, open up their imaginations, and create something meaningful out of nothing. It could be something that they could not say in any other way, something that perhaps they didn't know they even felt, something that found its way into a poem from a keepsake stored in their psyche that they won't ever forget.

Chapter One

Getting Serious about Poems
Middle School and High School

> *In a rundown part of town*
> *Or in the back of a wondering mind*
>
> —Mike, grade 12, *from* "Red Lamp District"

"First Gig," by Shelley Savren

I just arrived in town
barely getting the feel of sand
between my toes
the whiff of ocean salt
when I was sent
just like that
to a high school class
to replace another poet
and I was not much older
than those kids
with no idea
how to navigate that terrain
so I tried Beethoven's "Pastoral"
paintings and photographs
brought in Whitman
and in that opening
they began pulling out words
each week the ink oozing
bulging between lines
as they searched for images
under desks and chairs
in trash cans
poking out like ghosts

> through windows and doors
> and when they read their poems
> out loud there was rocking
> in the classroom
> raining from their throats
> a kaboom of words
> they never knew they kept inside

The California Poets in the Schools (CPITS) program began in San Francisco in 1964 but didn't start up in San Diego until 1975, and the following January, one of the first poetry-writing workshops was held at a high school there. At that time, there was no training program, and it was incumbent upon the visiting poet to rouse students' excitement.

Integrating music and art as part of the exercises seemed like a good idea, along with reading lots of poetry to the students. And as kids at all ages are flexible and often willing to try new things, those students began writing poetry, and miraculously, they loved it. Soon after that first high school workshop, it became easier to develop a curriculum, one that continued to evolve over several decades.

Getting middle and high school students to write poems is fairly easy, but when it comes to reading aloud, not everyone wants to participate. In some classrooms, students like to put on a show and share their work. But it's not unusual to have no volunteers. So sometimes students can just pair off and read what they wrote to each other.

Often students don't want to read their poems because they feel vulnerable or are afraid they'll get into trouble with someone. Some write about very personal things, such as boyfriends and girlfriends, first dates, and even sexual experiences. Others write about their parents, sometimes revealing a closeness and sometimes showing feelings of neglect or abandonment. Philip, a tenth grade student, wrote:

"At Nine"

> Born within her
> she leaves us
> leaving me with one
> thinking she will come back
> seven years, then a call
> she has died
> I'm sorry.

As the workshops progress, though, more and more students usually develop trust in the process, and more will begin to read aloud. The goal, though, is to keep them writing, to support their opening up, and to let them know it's okay if they don't want to share what they write.

When the residencies are short, students can revise and type up their poems at home and bring them back the following session. They learn that revision is a different kind of exercise than merely writing from inspiration. With revision, students have to figure out diction, rhythm, and form. They need to be of service to the poem, discovering what works best. And that takes time and persistence. When students revise their poems, they are not just exercising their creative skills; they're using critical-thinking skills, too. Revision has a kinship with mathematics because it employs problem-solving skills.

During longer residencies, students can pair off in partners and revise their poems together, or they can critique the poems as a class. It's crucial for the class to create a supportive environment, which means that every student's poem is critiqued honestly and fully. No one should go away feeling attacked or thinking that his or her poem was too "good" to get feedback. Every writer should be given suggestions that will help to know how the reader is receiving her or his poem. And students have to commit to being open to hearing responses.

Sometimes classmates just need to ask questions to get more information for the poem. Sometimes the poem just needs to be more specific or have a more provocative title. Students can use the following critiquing sheet and should be encouraged to be as specific as possible when giving feedback, to make suggestions but not attempt to edit the poem. That's the author's job.

STUDENTS CRITIQUING STUDENTS: SOME GUIDELINES FOR REVISION GROUPS

1. Have the author read the poem aloud.
2. Acknowledge the strengths of the poem.
    a. Find an image or line or even word that stands out.
    b. Look for strong details, colors, use of five senses.
3. Tell what you get from the poem in terms of meaning.
    a. Tell what confuses you, if anything.
    b. Look at the poem as a whole and evaluate what's working and what's not.
    c. Suggest changes in point of view or tense that might improve the poem.
    d. Suggest any rearrangement of lines or stanzas.
    e. Suggest any elimination of sections that don't enhance the poem.
    f. Look for areas that need to be more developed due to vagueness. Ask the poet questions that might prompt him or her to add more information.

4. Go through the poem line by line.
    a. Point out strengths, such as word choice, images, details, and the like.
    b. Point out areas that need to be eliminated, such as wordiness, abstractions, or clichés.
    c. Point out areas that can be strengthened by using images, metaphors, similes, or other figurative language.
5. Check to see if the poem flows rhythmically and suggest changes.
6. Check for line and stanza breaks. Look for strong words to begin and end lines.
7. Point out any spelling or grammar errors.
8. Check the form for natural breath lines.
9. Ask the author how he or she feels about the feedback.

Although revision becomes an important part of the process in those workshops, writing the poems themselves is paramount, because that's where the students get hooked. It's also important for students to read poetry outside of school. If they want to be good at writing poetry, they need to read quality poetry, often suggested by visiting poets or teachers. They also need to be encouraged to attend poetry readings in their communities and even read their poems at open mics. High school students can have their own readings in their communities, as well.

As a result of these particular poetry-writing workshops held at middle and high schools, mostly in San Diego and Ventura counties, for almost forty years, some students decided to major in English when they were ready for college. Some got poems published in their school newspapers and journals or in CPITS anthologies or even in literary magazines. Some won contests. Some read them on the radio or made audio or video recordings of themselves reading their poems.

But one of the greatest joys was when those students showed up at college creative writing classes at Oxnard College in Ventura County. They were serious about continuing on the journey. They were ready to embrace the craft.

SAMPLE WRITING EXERCISES

Part I: Middle School

1) Imagination and Empathy: Seeing the Person Behind the Portrait

First talk about the imagination. Then focus on the idea of imagination as a form of empathy. Ask the students to imagine what the person on the other side of an argument feels. Then ask them to imagine the life of someone they don't know and to think about what that person might think and feel and what the person's life might be like. The person can be someone very different from themselves, even from another culture that they know little about. Then read model poems.

"Surrounded by All the Falling," by Jane Hirshfield

After four days of rain
sunlight fills the branches like returning birds,
one of those flocks men believed
they could shoot at forever and never reach the end.
They went fluttering, one by one,
to extinction in seven years.
But this day startles in its sudden gold,
its colored persimmons, rust, and fallen
pine needles blond as a child's hair on the barber's floor;
the sound of his snipping businesslike and crisp.
When loss reaches her, she cannot even cry out,
But where has it gone?
And the sky, so utterly blue it can barely be faced.
It is time to plant bulbs again,
to fork and seed the empty beds into flower.
I turn to feel the sleep-warmth of your hands,
the even breathing that tells me you are close by—
it is still the only story that lets me wake content,
emerge from all the falling of dreams,
the crowded harbor of ships whose riggings
ring like bells,
dance like circus wires.

The girl slides down from the swiveling chair,
her hair combed to new curls.
Soon enough,
I can tell by this day's
windowed, blowsy beauty, it will begin to snow.
She will lie down in it, carefully move
her arms once up, once down

and rise to contemplate quietly, a long time,
the wings she has carved herself out of the cold.

Talk about how the speaker tries to imagine what the young girl might be feeling after she gets her hair cut. Then the speaker gets into her own childlike space and imagines the girl lying down and making snow angels, something that perhaps a young girl would do in the snow.

In the next poem, the speaker sees the beauty of a woman he calls "the queen." No one else recognizes this beauty, no matter where she goes. He is so taken by her that, by the end of the poem, he has fallen in love with her. If we picture this woman being watched by the speaker, we might imagine how she feels being the object of such love.

"The Queen," by Pablo Neruda, translated by Donald D. Walsh

I have named you queen.
There are taller ones than you, taller.
There are purer ones than you, purer.
There are lovelier than you, lovelier.

But you are the queen.

When you go through the streets
no one recognizes you.
No one sees your crystal crown, no one looks
at the carpet of red gold
that you tread as you pass,
the nonexistent carpet.

And when you appear
all the rivers sound
in my body, bells
shake the sky,
and a hymn fills the world.

Only you and I,
only you and I, my love,
listen to it.

Now it's time to write. Pass out pictures from magazines of people from all walks of life—definitely different from American preteens. *National Geographic* has great pictures. Ask the students to stretch their imaginations and make up a life for the person in their photo, to study the expression on his or her face and let that expression be an entryway to the person's life, joys, and worries. Ask them to imagine where the person lives, what she or he does, who his or her other family members are, what she or he likes to eat, and so forth.

When the students read their poems, hold up the pictures for everyone to see. Here's a student poem about the woman in her photo.

"Woman," by Addie, sixth grade

I see a woman. Night is on her shoulders,
rags on her soul.
She seems not to notice
and hums a spellbinding song.
She jumps into the river.

The water takes her to the Arctic.
She goes under not to be seen again.
The sunlight spills down her.
Cold surrenders to the warmth.
She thinks about something
important, nothing at all.
All the hours of hard work
have healed and she goes into
that wonderful place we call dreams.

2) Perception: The Five Senses and the Four Elements

Ask, "What would it be like to not be able to see? How would you describe the color of the sky? Or imagine not being able to hear. How would you describe the sound of a waterfall? Or imagine not being able to feel your boyfriend's or girlfriend's hand or smell or taste the food you eat. People usually don't think about this, but using the five senses makes what you write come alive."

Then talk about the four elements: earth, water, air, and fire. The world is made up of these things. People need them to live and be nourished; however, they can also be destructive. Earthquakes can bury whole towns, even civilizations; tsunamis can destroy buildings and drown people; tornado winds can blow down trees and houses; and fires can destroy whole forests.

Ask if anyone has ever witnessed a natural disaster. Several students will have stories to tell. After this discussion, read two model poems. Both poems show how the world changes as a result of the elements—rain and wind or just rain.

"Raining," by Eloise Klein Healy

Blowing, it was raining and I was standing
in a dry circle protected by a tree,
and there was so many leaves on that tree
the rain blowing didn't fall within the ring of its limbs
and the bark to a height of ten feet above my head was dry.

Blowing and raining, it was so stormy
that even under the shelter of a tree, the rain fell
between the leaves as they shook in the storm,
as they blew this way and that while the slender trunk
swayed side to side and the whole crown swung wildly.

Raining and blowing, the gusting wind whipped me.
The poor tree, a sapling really, no bigger around
than my arm and still trained between two poles

did nothing to protect me from the storm,
but I stood by it,
put myself between it and the wind
until nothing of me was dry, nothing of me safe
except that I had stood before in blowing rain
and would again,
and would again with no tree at all.

"Coping," by Audre Lorde

It has rained for five days
running
the world is
a round puddle
of sunless water
where small islands
are only beginning
to cope
a young boy
in my garden
is bailing out water
from his flower patch
when I ask him why
he tells me
young seeds that have not seen sun
forget
and drown easily.

Tell the students to imagine the enormity of the elements, to visualize their power and write from there. If they want to, they can tell a story about a natural disaster. Or they can just write about the element and the path it takes.

Here's a poem by a student about the element of fire. Discuss how it uses similes to describe the fire's actions and how it's written in four stanzas, the first and fourth being quatrains (four lines) and the middle two tercets (three lines).

"Fire," by Trisha, sixth grade

It engulfs the earth,
stealing hopes and lives.
It stretches up against the dark sky,
like the moon.

It waits behind a door,
like a snake waiting to strike.
Then it shows no mercy.

A black fog settles over a city.
Even if gone, it is still there.
It is just waiting.

It waits until the time is right.
Then it feeds itself, like an animal after a hunt.
It grows, bigger and stronger
until it's just a black void in the sky.

3) Emotions: Building Friendships and Partings

Talk about how expressing feelings is an essential ingredient in poetry. Then talk about friendships and ask the students to describe the qualities in a true friendship. Of course they will come up with a lot of abstractions. So ask them to go inside the abstractions and give real life examples. For instance, if they say that a friend is someone they can trust, ask them to describe a time when they trusted a friend and that friend came through for them.

Also talk about leaving friends. Sometimes they have to part with friends because one of them moves away. The friendship suffers and might not survive. Sometimes they feel abandoned by someone they love, and sometimes they lose someone because she or he dies. There are also good partings. For example, they can go to special places or on trips with their friends and leave other people behind. Then read model poems.

"Singing Back the World," by Dorianne Laux

I don't remember how it began.
The singing. Judy at the wheel
in the middle of *Sentimental Journey*.
The side of her face glowing.
Her full lips moving. Beyond her shoulder
the little houses sliding by.
And Geri. Her frizzy hair tumbling
in the wind wing's breeze, fumbling
with the words. All of us singing
as loud as we can. Off key.
Not even a semblance of harmony.
Driving home in a blue Comet singing
I'll Be Seeing You and *Love Is a Rose*.
The love songs of war. The war songs
of love. Mixing up verses, eras, words.
Songs from stupid musicals.
Coming in strong on the easy refrains.
Straining our middle aged voices
trying to reach impossible notes,
reconstruct forgotten phrases.

Cole Porter's *Anything Goes*.
Shamelessly la la la-ing
whole sections. Forgetting
the rent, the kids, the men,
the other woman. The sad goodbye.
The whole of childhood. Forgetting
the lost dog. Polio. The grey planes
pregnant with bombs. Fields
of white headstones. All of it gone
as we struggle to remember
the words. One of us picking up
where the others leave off. Intent
on the song. Forgetting our bodies,
their pitiful limbs, their heaviness.
Nothing but three throats
beating back the world—Laurie's
radiation treatments. The scars
on Christina's arms. Kim's brother.
Molly's grandfather. Jane's sister.
Singing to the telephone poles
skimming by. Stoplights
blooming green. The road,
a glassy black river edged
with brilliant gilded weeds. The car
an immense boat cutting the air
into blue angelic plumes. Singing
Blue Moon and *Paper Moon*
and *Mack the Knife*, and *Nobody Knows
the Trouble I've Seen.*

Here, the poet describes the women singing, "straining our middle aged voices," and they bond on their trip through singing, forgetting all of their woes in life. This next poem also shows a bonding, this time between two women who have been friends since childhood.

"For Jan, in Bar Maria," by Carolyn Kizer
in the style of Po Chü-i

Though it's true we were young girls when we met,
We have been friends for twenty-five years.
But we still swim strongly, run up the hill from the beach
                             without getting too winded.
Here we idle in Ischia, a world away from our birthplace—
That colorless town!—drinking together, sisters of summer.
Now we like to have groups of young men gathered around us.
We are trivial-hearted. We don't want to die any more.

Remember, fifteen years ago, in our twin pinafores
We danced on the boards of the ferry dock at Mukilteo
Mad as yearling mares in the full moon?
Here in the morning moonlight we climbed on a workman's cart
And three young men, shouting and laughing, dragged it up
                    through the streets of the village.
It is said we have shocked the people of Forio.
They call us Janna and Carolina, those two mad *straniere*.

The two female friends travel together to foreign countries, dance and flirt with men. The poet names foreign places and, in the end, refers to the speaker and her friend as strangers to others in Italy; yet the reader knows they're close friends to *each other*.

For this assignment, tell the students to describe a friendship, but more than that—to describe a time or times they spent together with a friend. Ask them to think about the following: What did they do? What did they talk about? What kind of adventures did they go on? What makes that person special? They could also describe the pain of having to leave that friend because of a fight or a move or something else that happened.

Here's a poem by a student that describes a friendship and all the special times they shared before one of them had to move away.

"Migrating Birds," by Talia, eighth grade
for Jessie

Big brown eyes flash
a wink
as a blue bubble pops
on your pale pink lips.

A yellow ball bounces
from square to square.
"Look at those third grade girls,
they're so big.
Do you think we'll be that big?"
you question me.

Ocean waves curl around you,
the sun kissing your skin.
Late, on the playground
we dig for Indian clay.
I find a plastic knife.
"That's mine!" a fourth grader shouts.

We sit outside the hospital.
Your brother, Marcus,
got hurt in the pool.

We make graves for him
just in case.

We never fight.
We're like soul mates,
you and me.

"You're my best friend, Talia,"
you say to me as we leave each other
and I move away.
The writing stops.
I don't understand.
We have gone our separate ways.

Me and you, Jess,
we're like migrating birds
flying north and south for the winter,
passing each other to say hello.

We live so close, yet so far.
I miss seeing you at school
sitting on the monkey bars
and teasing the boys.

We know how to say everything
except goodbye.

4) Imagery: Portraits of Grandparents

Talk about how imagery brings power and beauty to poems. It lifts the poem and holds it up for the reader to see. Poets can use imagery to create portraits of special people in their lives, particularly their grandparents. Many people spend special times with their grandparents, but the poet wants to make those times seem unique, particular to *her* or *his* grandparents—not just any grandparent. The goal is to put a picture in the reader's mind so that the grandparent described will stand out as unique. Then read model poems.

"The Sadness I Live For, by Patrice Vecchione
for Rose Vecchione

Grandmother's teeth sleep without her
in the blue box beside the bathroom sink
and greet me at night in their shiny silence
when I stumble across the aging floorboards
of grandmother's house.

Those porcelain teeth will outlast you, Grandma,
and without you they cannot speak

of traveling across Manhattan by horse,
of the boy born on the kitchen table,
or the tiny baby lost to influenza.
I can not fit those teeth into my own mouth
when you are gone, gone.

Early summer mornings, you wheel out
to the living room, your ancient half-legs
covered. Ghost of a woman,
you are my only hero. It's breakfast
and another television day beside the rumbling
air conditioner. I fall asleep in your presence,
dream of you, only twenty-five years ago,
the fine grandma you were, your homemade
spaghetti drying on the bed.

This year you will give me, maybe,
one more story, and I will ask for it, over
and over, again. I'll tell you stories of the family
I met last summer in the old country, the woman
who has grandpa's very own face, my skin, yours.

You'll hand me another string of pearls
left over from the thin years of tripe for dinner
or a bean soup, when you strung beads for money.
The fake strand will be longer this year,
as I am older, more deserving of your gems,
and the gold-threaded dresses I am too thin to wear.

Grandma, you are our history alive.
And when you are gone, you'll be more
than my hero; you'll be the end of a world,
the sadness I live for.

"The Morning Baking," by Carolyn Forché

Grandma, come back, I forgot
How much lard for these rolls

Think you can put yourself in the ground
Like plain potatoes and grow in Ohio?
I am damn sick of getting fat like you

Think you can lie through your Slovak?
Tell filthy stories about the blood sausage?
Pish-pish nights at the virgin in Detroit?

I blame your raising me up for my Slav tongue
You beat me up out back, taught me to dance

I'll tell you I don't remember any kind of bread
Your wavy loaves of flesh
Stink through my sleep
The stars on your silk robes

But I'm glad I'll look when I'm old
Like a gypsy dusha hauling milk

In both of these poems, the speakers are missing their grandmothers. In the poem by Patrice Vecchione, the speaker is sad to lose her grandmother. In the one by Carolyn Forché, the speaker reflects on how similar she is to her grandmother. Both poems tell stories of times the speakers spent with their grandmothers.

Now ask the students to write a poem using unique imagery to describe a grandparent and include a special time or times that they spent with him or her. If they don't have grandparents, they can think of an older relative or friend, like a neighbor, whom they spent time with. If they lost a grandparent, their poem can reflect that loss.

Here's a poem by a student that uniquely describes her grandmother and the special relationship that they have. What makes it especially strong is that she titles the poem with the name that she calls her grandmother, which is in Spanish. She also uses Spanish in the poem. Talk about the value of writing a bilingual poem and how it's not necessary to translate lines, since, as in this case, the Spanish can be understood in the context of the poem.

"Mamita," by Gaby, sixth grade

Mamita sits on her rocking chair
sewing a butterfly.
"*¿Qué estás haciendo, Mamita?*" I ask her.
She smiles and tells me to mind my business.
I go play.
Mamita sits making *tortillas* and *frijoles con chile*.
Mamita sings one of her favorite songs,
"*El Niño Dios.*"

Mamita sees me and holds her arms out.
I run toward her and kiss her.
Mamita goes to her room
and lies on her bed taking a little nap.
I go to her room but I don't see her.
She is on her other bed.
I try to wake her up.
She makes no moves whatsoever.
I tell my mama.

We both try to wake her up.
She is dead.

I never looked forward to this day.
It finally came.
"¿Mamita, por qué te fuiste?"
I cry when I see her.
Her skin is as white as the coffin she lies in.
Her wrinkles have gone pale
and her face is as cold as a blizzard.
Her face and skin are soft like rose petals.
I will always cherish the moment
of that special kiss that she gave me.
"Mamita, I will never forget you."

Sample Writing Exercises—Part II: High School

1) Imagination: Rewriting Fairy Tales

Talk about fairy tales and imagine them being written in poetry form. So much has been done with fairy tales in animated movies that the original writings are no longer what people know. But poets can play with those original stories. They can write from the perspective of the villain or the hero or heroine now grown-up. Poets can also imagine characters behaving differently than in the original stories or they can change a story's setting to modern times.

Ask students to volunteer to read the model poems. Begin with a long poem by Anne Sexton, where she rewrites the fairy tale of "Rapunzel," complete with commentary and contemporary references. The poem, part of her book *Transformations*, is very long, so just read this excerpt that tells the story.

from "Rapunzel," by Anne Sexton

Once there was a witch's garden
more beautiful than Eve's
with carrots growing like little fish,
with many tomatoes rich as frogs,
onions as ingrown as hearts,
the squash singing like a dolphin
and one patch given over wholly to magic—
rampion, a kind of salad root,
a kind of harebell more potent than penicillin,
growing leaf by leaf, skin by skin,
as rapt and as fluid as Isadora Duncan.

However the witch's garden was kept locked
and each day a woman who was with child
looked upon the rampion wildly,
fancying that she would die
if she could not have it.
Her husband feared for her welfare
and thus climbed into the garden
to fetch the life-giving tubers.

Ah ha, cried the witch,
whose proper name was Mother Gothel,
you are a thief and now you will die.
However they made a trade,
typical enough in those times.
He promised his child to Mother Gothel
so of course when it was born
she took the child away with her.
She gave the child the name Rapunzel,
another name for the life-giving rampion.
Because Rapunzel was a beautiful girl
Mother Gothel treasured her beyond all things.
As she grew older Mother Gothel thought:
None but I will ever see her or touch her.
She locked her in a tower without a door
or a staircase. It had only a high window.
When the witch wanted to enter she cried:
Rapunzel, Rapunzel, let down your hair.
Rapunzel's hair fell to the ground like a rainbow.
It was as yellow as a dandelion
and as strong as a dog leash.
Hand over hand she shinnied up
the hair like a sailor
and there in the stone-cold room,
as cold as a museum,
Mother Gothel cried:
Hold me, my young dear, hold me,
and thus they played mother-me-do.

Years later a prince came by
and heard Rapunzel singing her loneliness.
That song pierced his heart like a valentine
but he could find no way to get to her.
Like a chameleon he hid himself among the trees
and watched the witch ascend the swinging hair.
The next day he himself called out:
Rapunzel, Rapunzel, let down your hair,
and thus they met and he declared his love.

Each day he brought her a skein of silk
to fashion a ladder so they could both escape.
But Mother Gothel discovered the plot
and cut off Rapunzel's hair to her ears
and took her into the forest to repent.
When the prince came the witch fastened
the hair to a hook and let it down.
When he saw Rapunzel had been banished
he flung himself out of the tower, a side of beef.
He was blinded by thorns that prickled him like tacks.
As blind as Oedipus he wandered for years
until he heard a song that pierced his heart
like that long-ago valentine.
As he kissed Rapunzel her tears fell on his eyes
and in the manner of such cure-alls
his sight was suddenly restored.

They lived happily as you might expect
proving that mother-me-do
can be outgrown,
just as the fish on Friday,
just as a tricycle.
The world, some say,
is made up of couples.
A rose must have a stem.

As for Mother Gothel,
her heart shrank to the size of a pin,
never again to say: Hold me, my young dear,
hold me,
and only as she dreamt of the yellow hair
did moonlight sift into her mouth.

In this poem, the poet goes back to the original details of the fairy tale and uses her imagination to add clever descriptions to the poem. It's loaded with similes, for example, "carrots growing like little fish," "tomatoes rich as frogs," and so on.

In the next model poem, the fairy-tale characters in "Hansel and Gretel" have grown up, and Gretel has nightmares as she remembers the witch.

"Gretel in Darkness," by Louise Glück

This is the world we wanted.
All who would have seen us dead
are dead. I hear the witch's cry

break in the moonlight through a sheet
of sugar: God rewards.
Her tongue shrivels into gas. . . .

        Now, far from women's arms
and memory of women, in our father's hut
we sleep, are never hungry.
Why do I not forget?
My father bars the door, bars harm
from this house, and it is years.

No one remembers. Even you, my brother,
summer afternoons you look at me as though
you meant to leave,
as though it never happened.
But I killed for you. I see armed firs,
the spires of that gleaming kiln—

Nights I turn to you to hold me
but you are not there.
Am I alone? Spies
hiss in the stillness, Hansel,
we are there still and it is real, real,
that black forest and the fire in earnest.

    Ask the students which fairy tales they remember, and they will name several. Tell them to choose one and either rewrite it in poetry form with a new twist or change the setting. For example, Cinderella could go to the ball dressed in leather and riding a Harley. Or they could have the characters be grown up and tell what happens after "happily ever after." Snow White might be divorced, or her prince might be having an affair with one of the chambermaids.

    Or they could retell the story in poetry form from the point of view of the villain. For example, maybe the wolf in Little Red Riding Hood has a den of hungry cubs to feed, and so on. Here's a poem by a student taking the perspective of the villain—in this case, the wicked witch. The poem is full of compassion and shows an understanding for the one always labeled as bad.

"Why So Wicked," by John, twelfth grade

How simple it is to say
that in perspective lies happiness
when joy can be exchanged with friends.
But what of those who have no one,
whose laughter is never heard?

Changing one's ways is said to be hard,
even harder without any help.

But imagine awaking in the dark, gloomy castle
knowing only the walls are there to listen,
that even the moat monsters are indifferent.

Who could manage a smile to the morning
knowing the sun shines for others
and the birds sing only sorrow?

2) Perception: Writing to Classical Music

Talk about why it's important for students to use their five senses in a poem. Tell them that a poem can be very sensual and can arouse someone's hunger or make a person want to run and feel the earth or squeeze a boyfriend's hand or watch a girlfriend dance. These things make a poem come alive.

Then talk about music as an obvious use of one of the senses. But while listening to the sounds in music, they can imagine their other senses coming into play. Music can also take people on a journey in their imaginations. Some music, especially classical music, is dreamlike, and someone can float along through that dream and see what happens. Tell the students that they're going to write to classical music using their five senses, but first have students volunteer to read a model poem and then a student poem.

In the poem by Perie Longo, the speaker imagines going fishing with her father. She remembers how much she loved being with him, and now she misses him and imagines being with him. In the untitled poem by the student, the speaker is in a dreamlike state searching for someone and is eventually traveling with him. Both poems use the five senses, especially sight, sound, and touch.

"Fishing with my Father," by Perie Longo

He always took me with him out in the boat
on those long northern summer nights
and I loved it, not the sitting for hours
under all the many moons and showy red lights,
but the going—the creak of oars in the locks
like entering an attic where no one could reach us,
water beads on the edge of the oar
like a string of pearls before they dripped back
into the mirror that held us all.
I realize now how many poems I thought up
in those hours while we stared the bobber down
praying for a catch. I used to play games to pass the time,
for it was not the fishing that pleased me
but being with my father
in his joy. If I blinked my eyes thirty-nine times,

on the fortieth a Muskie would strike,
that fish he took to heaven I think.
When I held his arm at his passing,
clung to his hand like no fish ever had,
he let go and I slipped off.
If I blink thirty-nine times, on the fortieth
maybe I'll catch a glimpse of him.

"Untitled," by Ashley, twelfth grade

As if in a dream I glide through the night
like a blind dog on a leash
guided by my heart. He doesn't know
I am coming yet, I don't know
why I am looking for him. I have
to find him, there is no choice in
the matter, it is not my choice.
When our eyes finally meet
in a calm embrace, invisible
earthquakes in our hearts, our souls,
shaking away the past.
The conforming walls of expectation
crumbling to nothingness,
all that remains is our pure hearts on the path
to togetherness, the road we had been
waiting for, but didn't recognize
until we were there.
And now we will travel together
because we found each other.
But we know now,
we were in each other all along.

Next, play part of "Pastoral," the Sixth Symphony by Ludwig van Beethoven, throughout the writing period. Any other piece of tranquil classical music will also do. Tell the students to listen for about five minutes and imagine that they are somewhere or with someone or searching for the perfect time or place. Suggest that they allow the music to take them on a journey and imagine what they can see, touch, taste and, of course, hear. They can enter a meditative state by closing their eyes before they write if they want.

Here's a poem by a student who imagines a place and a time with someone she loved. She also uses the senses of sight and sound.

"Someday," by Melinda, tenth grade

Someday is a place, a time, a dream,
a blade of grass,

dried out and remembering.
A day when someday was reality
and filled with hope.

Someday was a word
we used to tease each other,
a distant spot.
But we were anxious
trying to find too much too soon.

Someday was a dream,
a boy I knew and loved
in a someday sort of way,
because today was never
quite his style.

Someday was a child
we would have had
but didn't.
A time I knew would come
but never has.

3) Emotions: First-Time Experience—Facing the Truth

Discuss how essential it is to express emotions in poems. That's the real reason most people write poetry. Once someone embraces the craft, then writing poems takes on another purpose: to create art. But without expressing feelings, the poem becomes an exercise in using language. There is a place for "language poetry," but that's not what these poetry workshops are about.

Then talk about first-time experiences and how they make people face the truth. People lose their innocence and know something about life that they hadn't realized before. They grow up, become responsible, and can never go back to the way they were. Next, ask for a student volunteer to read the first model poem.

"Snowy Egret," by Bruce Weigl

My neighbor's boy has lifted his father's shotgun and stolen
down to the backwaters of the Elizabeth
and in the moon he's blasted a snowy egret
from the shallows it stalked for small fish.

Midnight. My wife wakes me. He's in the backyard
with a shovel so I go down half drunk with pills
that let me sleep to see what I can see and if it's safe.
The boy doesn't hear me come across the dewy grass.

He says through tears he has to bury it,
he says his father will kill him
and he digs until the hole is deep enough and gathers
the egret carefully into his arms
as if not to harm the blood-splattered wings
gleaming in the flashlight beam.

His man's muscled shoulders
shake with the weight of what he can't set right no matter what,
but one last time he tries to stay a child, sobbing
please don't tell. . . .
He says he only meant to flush it from the shadows,
he only meant to watch it fly
but the shot spread too far
ripping into the white wings
spanned awkwardly for a moment
until it glided into brackish death.

I want to grab his shoulders,
Shake the lies loose from his lips but he hurts enough,
he burns with shame for what he's done,
with fear for his hard father's
fists I've seen crash down on him for so much less.
I don't know what to do but hold him.
If I let go he'll fly to pieces before me.
What a time we share, that can make a good boy steal away,
wiping out from the blue face of the pond
what he hadn't even known he loved, blasting
such beauty into nothing.

Talk about the poem and the story it tells from the point of view of the neighbor. Clearly, there is the message of child abuse. The speaker knows that this boy is not a bad kid, and he has compassion for him. The boy loses his innocence as revealed in the lines, "His man's muscled shoulders/shake with the weight of what he can't set right no matter what/but one last time he tries to stay a child, sobbing."

Also point out the interesting twist of language in the beginning: "My neighbor's boy has lifted his father's shotgun and stolen/down to the backwaters of the Elizabeth." The boy *stole* the shotgun, but the poet writes that the boy "lifted" the shotgun, so he could use the word "stolen" in a different way. Then ask a volunteer to read the next model poem.

"Bird Grieves for the Man They Killed," by Elijah Imlay

We wore the steel bracelets
of Montagnards—money

for that mountain people,
good fortune for us. I held
my broken glasses together
with safety pins. I wrote
the 23rd Psalm on my helmet's
elastic band. John Jim,
our ammo bearer, gave us
each a Navajo necklace,
turquoise and onyx
with single white feather,
strung by his wife. I took out
earphones every night
and listened to George Harrison
sing *My Sweet Lord*. If only
we had not found a picture
of wife or girlfriend
in the billfold of the Vietnamese
we killed. Easy to say
it wasn't me who shot him,
but I still see his eyes
that never close and should
accuse me, yet don't.
They're looking at her photo.

In this poem the speaker, named "Bird," has to face the truth about what happened during the Vietnam War. Talk about how anyone who goes to war loses his or her innocence. In this case, the American soldier killed a Vietnamese soldier. Bird actually wasn't even sure if it was *his* shot that killed the Vietnamese man. But when Bird saw a picture of the dead man's wife or girlfriend in his wallet, Bird recognized the other soldier's humanity. Here was a young man, just like him, who loved a woman. At that moment, Bird lost his innocence.

Now it's time to write. Ask the students to think of an experience that had a profound effect on them when growing up, when they had to face the truth about something. It could be a good first-time experience, like hitting a home run, or a regretful experience, like stealing from a store. Tell them to allow the experience to capture the emotion without stating it, as in the poems they just read.

Here's a marvelous poem by a student describing the atmosphere where the speaker's first kiss took place. The student poet builds a sensual poem, beginning with a physically cold night, then the sound of music, the sight of dancing, the sweat of bodies, the feel of lights, the feel of "her arms/on his shoulders" and the look of "his dark brown eyes/on her face." In the end, it's the raven who steals the kiss, and "a trace of innocence [is] lost."

"First Kiss," by Mabel, eleventh grade

The cold, dark night
releases its malignant
pure evil . . .
an essence
that brings pleasure
to a lonely heart.

There is movement all around
from those ready
to devour the lamb . . .
prepare the sacrifice.
They dance to the music
intense . . .
thrilling . . .
tempting . . .

Two sweaty bodies nearly touch.
They dance
absorbing the heat
of the moment.

Luminescent
changing colored lights
ricochet off savages
or rather those
consciously unaware
of the passion
which fills the air.

Her arms
on his shoulders,
his dark brown eyes
on her face.

The music drums its beat . . .
a fire begins to burn . . .
the raven steals a kiss.
A trace of innocence . . . lost.

4) Imagery: Getting Lost Inside Ourselves, an Object, or a Concept

First discuss how imagery is the language of poetry where words become pictures. Then talk about images of the self, how people can get lost inside themselves or find themselves reflected in other people they know or in experiences that they've had. They can even find something of themselves in objects, like keepsakes, or in "concept words" that apply to themselves.

For example, if a boy wears a jacket all the time, that particular jacket will remind people of that boy. Or if someone is a bully, the concept of "meanness" will come to mind when people think of that person. Then ask a student to volunteer to read a model poem.

"Iris," by David St. John
Vivian St. John (1891–1974)

There is a train inside this iris:

You think I'm crazy, & like to say boyish
& outrageous things. No, there is

A train inside this iris.
It's a child's finger bearded in black banners.
A single window like a child's nail,

A darkened porthole lit by the white, angular face

Of an old woman, or perhaps the boy beside her in the stuffy,
Hot compartment. Her hair is silver, & sweeps

Back off her forehead, onto her cold & bruised shoulders.

The prairies fail along Chicago. Past the five
Lakes. Into the black woods of her New York; & as I bend

Close above the iris, I see the train

Drive deep into the damp heart of its stem, & the gravel
Of the garden path

Cracks under my feet as I walk this long corridor

Of elms, arched
Like the ceiling of a French railway pier where a boy

With pale curls holding

A fresh iris is waving goodbye to a grandmother, gazing
A long time

Into the flower, as if he were looking some great

Distance, or down an empty garden path & he believes a man
Is walking toward him, working

Dull shears in one hand; & now believe me: The train

Is gone. The old woman is dead, & the boy. The iris curls,
On its stalk, in the shade

Of those elms: Where something like the icy & bitter fragrance

In the wake of a woman who's just swept past you on her way
Home

& you remain.

The speaker in this poem is a boy who is looking into an iris that reminds him of his grandmother and how she left on a train when he was young. But now his grandmother has died and he has grown up. The poet uses wonderful images in the poem, such as "there is a train inside this iris" and "I see the train/Dive deep into the black heart of its stem . . ." and "a fresh iris is waving goodbye to a grandmother . . ." and "like the icy & bitter fragrance." The whole concept of looking into an iris and seeing a train with a grandmother on it is a great image in itself.

Then ask another student to read another model poem.

"Kindness," by Naomi Shihab Nye

Before you know what kindness really is
you must lose things,
feel the future dissolve in a moment
like salt in a weakened broth.
What you held in your hand,
what you counted and carefully saved,
all this must go so you know
how desolate the landscape can be
between the regions of kindness.
How you ride and ride
thinking the bus will never stop,
the passengers eating maize and chicken
will stare out the window forever.

Before you learn the tender gravity of kindness,
you must travel where the Indian in a white poncho
lies dead by the side of the road.
You must see how this could be you,
how he too was someone
who journeyed through the night with plans
and the simple breath that kept him alive.

Before you know kindness as the deepest thing inside,
you must know sorrow as the other deepest thing.
You must wake up with sorrow.
You must speak to it till your voice
catches the thread of all sorrows
and you see the size of the cloth.

Then it is only kindness that makes sense anymore,
only kindness that ties your shoes

and sends you out into the day to mail letters and purchase bread,
only kindness that raises its head
from the crowd of the world to say
It is I you have been looking for,
and then goes with you everywhere
like a shadow or a friend.

Here, the poet uses the similes "like salt in a weakened broth" to show how something can dissolve and "like a shadow or a friend" to show how kindness follows a person. There are other images such as "the tender gravity of kindness" and "only kindness that ties your shoes." In this last image, the poet uses personification, giving human characteristics to the concept of kindness. The meaning of kindness is in the person who experiences it, who finds kindness inside herself or himself when nothing else "makes sense anymore."

Ask the students to look for themselves inside someone else or inside an object or a concept, such as in the poems they just read, and write poems with images that reflect upon a memory, an experience, or just a description of who they are.

Here's a poem by a student who is chasing someone desperately. When he catches him and begins to hurt him, he realizes that he's killing himself. The poem is a revelation of who the speaker really is—someone "unfamiliar/. . . hair dark and long/Like a horse's mane," which is also a great simile. The message is that often people run away from or fight themselves.

"The Chase," by Frank, twelfth grade

As it begins I am going
After him once again.
His name, his face, unfamiliar.
His hair dark and long
Like a horse's mane.
He is running away from me,
Down a canyon
And into a dark, misty cave.
A feeling of joy hits me
As I sense him trapped.

I catch him
And he strains to get away.
I grab him by the neck
As if to pull his larynx out.
His head still down,
I pull it up by his hair.
Terror rushes through my body
As I scream with fear.
I am killing myself.

Chapter Two

Can Words Save Me?

Teens with Mental Health Issues

My poem doesn't know me.

If it knew me
it wouldn't show itself.

It taunts me with
every line.

It constantly eats
at my fingers.

—*from* "Poem from Hell" by Karlson, 12th grade

"Priscilla's Journal," by Shelley Savren

There's this school
with locks on every door. These meds.
Placement homes for foster kids
with closets full of neckties
bathroom cans of shaving cream and blades
cabinets with Tylenol, basement bar and bottles of gin
older boys who jump me in the dark
belts, long enough for every loop in my dad's pants
windows, second stories, alleys and concrete.
But at this school I have my notebook and my poems.
There's the time-in room, a counselor and a couch.
I can cry and everyone will hear me.
If I'm lucky when I turn 18
I can go to college or a halfway house or shelter
and when I'm lonely, walk the streets.
I can paint a mural on the liquor store.

I can sneak into my boyfriend's house for speed.
I can break a window just to breathe
and let out all my screams.

Teaching poetry to teens with mental illnesses is often viewed as therapy. Sometimes these students are difficult, to say the least, are not particularly likeable, and are often outcasts from their world and from most of society. But somewhere inside of them their imaginations are waiting for a spark, something that will allow them to open up and forget they are considered crazy or an opportunity to embrace that craziness and announce it proudly. Great artists are not afraid to live on the edge, and these teens just need permission to express themselves in any way they want through poetry.

Phoenix School in Ventura, California, was a last resort for students who could not function in regular classrooms. Their academic skills ranged from special education to gifted, and in some cases, they were extremely gifted, but suicidal. Each classroom had only eight students, a teacher, and a paraeducator.

There were on-site mental health professionals and psychotherapists who pulled out students and counseled them individually and in groups. Almost every single student was on medication, and it was obvious from his or her behavior when the meds needed to be adjusted.

It was the new millennium, and the teachers all used behavior modification to control their classes. Every student's name was on a chart ranking her or his behavior from "soaring" to try "harder." One day, a student was locked in the time-in room, pounding the walls and screaming, with a mental health professional trying to calm him down. This was not at all an unusual occurrence. Some students buried their heads and refused to write or participate. And some couldn't write enough and even brought in poems they had written at home.

In a structured environment like this, the goal is to somehow reach the students through poetry, to get them to express themselves—to write anything at all. But of course, the ultimate goal is to get them to love poetry as a friend.

Interestingly, these students often like to read the model poems aloud, and it's great to hear their voices. But when it comes time to write, it's important to circulate, sitting down next to every single student, getting him or her to open her or his poetry notebook and write. That means speaking with students privately about their ideas for poems and helping them get started.

Sometimes students will refuse to write to the prompt. It's their way of rebelling, and that was just fine. They might want to talk about what's going on that day, so suggest that they write about that. When they really don't want to write, it's okay. As the workshop progresses, most of the students will be eager to write poems addressing the open-ended assignment, and many will want to read their poems aloud.

On one occasion at Phoenix School, a student had been disturbing the class all morning, and his therapist was called in to remove him from the classroom and counsel him. But when that student saw that a poetry workshop was beginning, he went screaming down the hall, "I want to go to poetry." Ten minutes later he was back, attentive, on his best behavior and writing a poem.

For some students, writing poems was a lifesaver. Although it wasn't presented as therapy, it was exactly that. It was a place to turn to when they had their bouts of depression or were hyper or suicidal or whatever they suffered from. Jessica wrote: "I cut my wrists/I cut to the bone." Diandra wrote: "Now it looks just like this:/dark skin, curly hair, long legs, reaching arms./Wow! Loneliness looks just like Me!"

A few wrote about abuse at home. Yet most students wrote about the same stuff that any other teens wrote about, like friendships. Jessica wrote, "She has the power/to put a smile on my face./She shows me the light on a rainy day."

There were two girls in particular, Priscilla and Amanda, who wrote constantly. They always came to class with new poems that they had written at home. When the workshops ended, the principal said that he didn't know what they would do without poetry workshops. It was a healing force in their lives, and they wrote with desperation.

About a year after the workshops ended, both Priscilla and Amanda appeared in downtown Ventura on separate occasions. Both were eighteen at that point and were no longer attending Phoenix School. Amanda was working at a clothing store. She was stable on her meds and was moving forward with her life with great success.

Amanda was excited and came running over to hug the visiting poet who had impacted her life. She wanted to share that she had a boyfriend, was going to community college, and was majoring in English. And she was writing poetry—every single day.

Several months later, Priscilla was walking around downtown Ventura looking for food. She was also excited to share a hug. When asked how she was doing, she replied, "Great!" For her, "great" had an interesting meaning. She was living at the river bottom. She could have been getting help from the county. They had a transition program for young adults like her. But she wanted nothing to do with the system. She'd rather be homeless and not on meds than have to follow any kind of structured protocol.

Survival had another meaning now. She took a doggie bag offered to her, making extra sure that it was okay, then walked away, opening the box of food, heading toward the riverbed. But before she turned the corner, she looked back and yelled, "I still have my poetry notebook." It was great to know that at least poetry still had a place in her life.

SAMPLE WRITING EXERCISES

1) Imagination: Becoming an Animal—Poems of Survival

Talk about how all poems, all creativity, comes from the imagination. Point out how the imagination helps in so many ways: *It's real; it's make-believe; it helps people make decisions; it's a survival tool; it helps people to empathize; it allows people to have visions; it creates dreams; it precedes invention and discovery; it's the key to freedom. People create with it; everyone uses it constantly.*

Then introduce the concept of a persona. A lot of students know that it means "person" in Spanish, but tell them that it has a different meaning in poetry. It means writing from someone else's point of view, and it goes beyond empathy because the poet doesn't just feel for the person; he or she *becomes* that person and feels *with* him or her. Actors have to do this when they perform. It can also be done with animals, imagining what it's like to be a dog or lion or goat or bird and what they need to do to survive.

Ask students to volunteer to read model poems. The first poem doesn't identify a specific animal, but it's obvious that it's one that lives in the wild.

"Explanation," by Molly Fisk

Finally I just gave up and became an animal.
I slept when I was tired,
sometimes dropping in mid-stride,
curling into a knot on the sunny floor.
I ate raw food at odd hours,
wiped my mouth on the back of my hand,
stopped brushing my hair.
The phone rang, but I didn't answer it.
Mail lay unopened on the stairs. Flowers
drooped in dry pots. Dust sifted down
from the ceiling in hazy swirls.
I left the windows open.
After a few weeks I grew
accustomed to it, sank deeper
into my actual body, learned to love
the hours as they passed.
I let go of the spinning
human world and walked in the hills at night
under a changing moon.
Deer swung their heads toward me.
I sat beside them in their beds of creaking grass
listening to crickets ticking in the heat.
I cooled my skin in the ocean, licked

the crusted salt from my arms.
In time, my throat forgot to speak,
it lost the bright angles of consonants,
the dark sloping vowels. I joined the chorus
of mute life with a kind of hum.

Here, the speaker gradually becomes a wild animal, eating raw food and licking salt from her arms, but the poem begins in her house, where she ignores her mail and just drops on the floor like an animal when she's tired and wants to sleep. That's what she needs to do in order to survive. In the next model poem, the speaker becomes a bird.

from "**Washington Square,**" **by Gerald Stern**

Now after all these years I am just that one pigeon
limping over toward that one sycamore tree
with my left leg swollen and my left claw bent and my neck
just pulling me along. It is the annual
day of autumn glory, but I am limping
into the shade of that one sycamore tree.

Note how the speaker imagines being a pigeon, experiencing how the pigeon walks, limping with its head bent. Now it's time to write. Ask the students to use their imaginations and become a wild animal and live inside that animal's skin, smelling what it smells, behaving as it does, feeling what it does, and encountering survival difficulties.

Here's a poem by a student where the speaker transforms into a werewolf. In the end, it's clear that the wolf has feelings for a girl who knows him as a human. Still, he's happier as a wolf, and that's what helps him to survive.

"Night Celebration," by Karlson, 12th grade

   I step into the night

All thoughts behind me.

   I step into the forest
My human shape behind
       me.

I cast off the world's
      banality
From thoughts like an
      ocean

   I throw away my worries
With only thoughts of a lycan.

> I search for my first
> > pleasure
> The only kill this night.
>
> I thrust my body towards
> With all my will-thrust might.
>
> I search for my lifelong
> > companion
> A thought of lust forms the
> > > gulf:
>
> I shall howl for you
> > Human girl.
>
> I shall know you in my human
> > skin
> But I will rejoice as a wolf.

2) Imagery and Personification: Shadows in Our Lives

Talk about images creating vivid pictures that people can see, hear, feel, or smell, making readers feel like they are there in the poem. Also talk about personification, giving human characteristics to nonhuman things. Then talk about shadows. Tell the students that their shadows can be their reflections, but they are slanted and aren't real. They also change, depending on the time of day. Shadows can follow people or lead them. Some shadows can be scary, and some can be playful. Regardless, shadows know where a person goes and what he or she does.

So that students don't think that you are encouraging them to just write dark poems, have a student read a fun poem with silly images like "My shadow wears/leopard shoes." The poet also uses personification, because the shadow becomes a person.

"My Shadow," by Susan Wooldridge

> My shadow wears
> leopard shoes
> ocean dress
> leopard hat
> and she knows
> the order of things. Her hair
> is green vines
> and she lives
> to drive men wild,
> they walk babbling into the sea.
> The mousier I act

the more men she drowns.
My shadow is a grey cat
who makes lizards drop
their frenzied tails
and makes me
wear her
shoes.

Next, ask a volunteer to read a student poem, also on the theme of shadows. This one is a little darker. The images appear in shadows.

"The Canyon," by Jeremy, 9th grade

Lonely and Bare
    Dark and Brown
        Shadows

A man
A while
To get home

Hold up the poem and point out the interesting form and the sparseness of language. The student poet is describing a canyon and a man walking. The reader can only see his shadow, not the man's features, and he's far from civilization out in this wilderness. But the poem doesn't tell us this. It only says, "A while/To get home."

Ask the students to write poems with images and somehow use the idea of shadows. They can be scary or playful. It can be their own shadow or anyone else's. They can also use personification if they'd like.

Here's a poem by a student that uses shadows as a place where depression comes creeping. She doesn't personify the shadow, but rather personifies the depression, using lines like: "You know it's there, rocking back and forth on its toes" and "He slashes at you, cuts that run deep."

"Depression," by Courtney, 11th grade

It comes creeping in the shadows.
You know it's there, rocking back and forth on its toes,
waiting to engulf you and drag you down.
You know it's there, waiting, watching,
staring you down, boring holes in you
with its eyes.
You know it's there. Inevitable, suffering madness:
chaos that doesn't cease,
a never-ending cycle.
The nightmare comes true.

He slashes at you, cuts that run deep
immense pain
a never-ending cycle.
His hands grab your throat.
No breathing, no seeing, no more being.
The nightmare comes true.

3) Details: Family Secrets—What We See and What We Realize

Discuss how details help the reader to understand what's going on in a poem and to imagine the picture. Then talk about family secrets and how they become more vivid when they have lots of details. Every family has secrets. Sometimes people are embarrassed about something or someone in their family or they just don't want other people to know about their family. Yet sometimes they want to expose them in poems.

Then read a model poem that takes the reader to a family gathering and fond memories. But the poem also gives the reader a peek into what's to come in the future, some not-so-happy times.

"Easter Sunday, 1955," by Elizabeth Spires

Why should anything go wrong in our bodies?
Why should we not be all beautiful? Why should
there be decay?—why death?—and, oh, why, damnation?
                                            —Anthony Trollope, in a letter

What were we? What have we become?
Light fills the picture, the rising sun,
the three of us advancing, dreamlike,
up the steps of my grandparents' house on Oak Street.
My mother and father, still young, swing me
lightly up the steps, as if I weighed nothing.
From the shadows, my brother and sister watch,
wanting their turn, years away from being born.
Now my aunts and uncles and cousins
gather on the shaded porch of generation,
big enough for everyone. No one has died yet.
No vows have been broken. No words spoken
that can never be taken back, never forgotten.
I have a basket of eggs my mother and I dyed yesterday.
I ask my grandmother to choose one, just one,
and she takes me up—O hold me close!—
her cancer not yet diagnosed. I bury my face
in soft flesh, the soft folds of her Easter dress,
breathing her in, wanting to stay forever where I am.

Her death will be long and slow, she will beg
to be let go, and I will find myself, too quickly,
in the here-and-now moment of my fortieth year.
It's spring again. Easter. Now my daughter steps
into the light, her basket of eggs bright, so bright.
One, choose one, I hear her say, her face upturned
to mine, innocent of outcome. Beautiful child,
how thoughtlessly we enter the world!
How free we are, how bound, put here in love's name
—death's, too—to be happy if we can.

Discuss the details in this poem. It begins with the speaker, a young child, going up the steps of her grandmother's house, remembering when "My mother and father, still young, swing me." She also fondly remembers burying her "face/in soft flesh, the soft folds of her [grandmother's] Easter dress."

Throughout the poem, there are glimpses of the future, for example, "No vows have been broken. No words spoken/that can never be taken back, never forgotten." This is a family secret. Someone will be unfaithful in a marriage. And the speaker of the poem, still a little girl, does not yet know that her grandmother's "death will be long and slow, and she will beg/to be let go. . . ."

Next, a volunteer reads a model poem that is written in one stanza with four long sentences. Ask the students to listen to the long breath lines that create a certain rhythm with lots of details.

"The Portrait," by Stanley Kunitz

My mother never forgave my father
for killing himself,
especially at such an awkward time
and in a public park,
that spring
when I was waiting to be born.
She locked his name
in her deepest cabinet
and would not let him out,
though I could hear him thumping.
When I came down from the attic
with the pastel portrait in my hand
of a long-lipped stranger
with a brave moustache
and deep brown level eyes,
she ripped it into shreds
without a single word
and slapped me hard.

In my sixty-fourth year
I can feel my cheek
still burning.

Ask the students which details they found to be most striking and memorable, and they might name the following lines: "She locked his name/in her deepest cabinet," "though I could hear him thumping," "a long-lipped stranger," "deep brown level eyes," and "I can feel my cheek/still burning." Then ask what the speaker was feeling. Everyone will agree that he was in pain. "From the slap?" you ask. No. They might say that the speaker is hurting because he knows nothing about his father, and his mother will never tell him. It's a secret.

Point out how the details in the poem lead to an emotion. Ask how the poem made them feel. A discussion might ensue about missing fathers and mothers in their lives. Some students will be able to relate to this theme; those who can't can imagine it.

The assignment is to write about a family secret. They can pick which details to use to describe a person or situation. The secret doesn't have to be an embarrassing one, either. It can be funny, or it can even be made up. For example, someone's grandma broke her arm surfing, or someone's aunt went to church in her nightgown. Or it can be serious, like someone got a divorce or had a heart attack or went to prison. Tell them to be creative and make up details that they don't know or can't remember.

Here's a poem by a student that's on the light side. He compares his grandfather to a dragon, but honors that symbol as one of bravery and loyalty. The secret is that his grandpa is also grumpy, but the speaker loves him anyway.

"Like a Dragon," by Scott, 10th grade

You say he's like a dragon
fierce and mean. But what I
see is what a dragon symbol
means. Bravery and loyalty. That's
what I see, see him helping
and loving, a little grumpy maybe.
But I love my grandpa
like a dragon.

4) Feelings: Forgiving, Loving, and Celebrating Our Friends and Ourselves

Ask: "What happens to you when you read a poem? Do you ever feel like you can relate to what's happening, even if your experience is different?" Talk about how sometimes people feel badly about themselves or their friends.

They have a hard time forgiving themselves for things they've done or forgiving their friends for things *they've* done.

The best thing they can do is turn it all around—forgive their friends and themselves and celebrate their lives. They can think about what's special about their lives, why they are special. If nothing else, they can think about how special it is that they write poems. Ask a student to read a model poem where the speaker realizes that she can start over and have wonderful things in her life. In that vein, it's a poem of celebration of sorts.

"The New House," by Glenna Luschei

We'll turn over new leaves.
Oak floors will be polished,
the oak table will gleam.

We'll sow the yard in clover
I'll build hives for the bees
hutches for rabbits
runs for chukars.

The oak table will gleam.

I'll tie up raspberry vine
with old silk hose
and mulch the roses with peat.

In this house we'll live forever
tablets behind our beds:
Here lie two grown children
with children of their own.

Oak floors will be polished,
the oak table will gleam.

Here, the speaker turns to hope, focusing on what the future will be in a new house. The poem lists positive, empowering things that the family can do in the new house, like "sow the yard in clover/. . . build hives for the bees/hutches for rabbits." The details show how happiness can be achieved.

Then have a student read a poem by another student where the speaker has mixed feelings about himself and how he should behave. The poem uses two wolves as metaphors for his good and bad behaviors and examines all aspects, but in the end the speaker's insight shows human strengths and weaknesses.

"A Fight within Myself," by Kyle, 9th grade

I always have a fight within myself.
It's like two wolves.
One is my good nature

the one that wants me to study,
to do my chores,
to be nice to my mom and dad,
to listen to them.
The other one
wants me to sneak out,
stay up late,
drink, act on my lust,
do drugs.
The two wolves battle
every time I have to make a decision.
I once told someone this
and they asked which one would win.
I told them,
"The one that I give my strength to."

Now it's time to write poems where students look at what's important in their lives and to allow their feelings to come through. They can either forgive themselves or a friend in their poem or celebrate their lives or something special in it, or the poem can do both.

Here's a poem by a student describing a friend in great detail. He uses punk language, which sounds negative, but is meant to be affectionate. But in the end, forgiveness and loss come through when the speaker misses his friend.

"Evan," by Andy, 12th grade

He rests on a couch by a wall,
his drink in his hand. He chuckles obnoxiously.
Studded denim, tight jeans, a black eye.
They make him look somewhat ridiculous.
He reminds me of Sid Vicious;
his hair is poofy and he always sneers.
what a dirty, crusty rock star.
He is making his guitar sound like a bulldozer,
for he has been drinking all day.
So skinny, it's like he has an eating disorder.
The man is nearly dead.
I miss the scumbag.

Chapter Three

Does Anybody Love Me?
Working with Incarcerated Youth

Part I: Girls' Rehabilitation Facility (GRF)

> *Inside these walls behind these gates*
> *my life is filled with misery.*
> *I sit in my room and look out my window*
> *and watch the birds as they fly by*
> *realizing they're free and I'm not.*
>
> —Cynthia, eighth grade

"She Wanted Vegas," by Shelley Savren

Thirteen and a runaway.
She ended up in the Hall and I found her
in a holding tank, blonde hair mashed down,
mouth open like a scar.

She wrote every day, about making out
with older boys in basements, walking the strip
in mini skirts, fishnet stockings and high,
high heels. How her feet hurt.

. . . .

She wrote about her grandparents' house,
smell of sauerkraut in the kitchen, German words
she couldn't pronounce.

Easter was her pre-release and her plot to AWOL.
She took her poems with her.

It is both rewarding and essential to teach poetry writing to young people who are considered "at risk"—particularly incarcerated teens. Most teens who get into trouble come from problematic homes and are frequently victims of abuse. The goal in working with this population is to reach them through poetry, to give them a creative way to express their anger, fears, hopes, or whatever else they are holding inside. Even if their writing has to be kept a secret, at least that secret can be written down in a poem that they don't have to show to anyone, not even the teacher or visiting poet.

From the beginning, it's important to establish a support system. Set ground rules for positive responses. These students have had enough negative criticism in their lives, so only complimentary feedback on their poems should be allowed. The goal is to get them to feel good about what they write, so they'll want to write more.

That goal was realized at the Sierra Vista High School GRF in San Diego. From 1977 to 1989, poetry-writing workshops were held at GRF for one hour twice a week. Poetry writing became part of the language arts curriculum, and both the teacher and the students loved it.

GRF was a lockdown facility, and the juvenile court sentenced girls there for up to a year. Most of them were in high school, but a few eighth graders were there as well. Typical crimes were: running away from home, truancy, breaking curfew, burglary, drug abuse, and violation of probation.

In 1977 few of them were in gangs, and many were guilty of reacting to crimes against them, such as physical or sexual abuse. Often, if there was incest in the family, instead of removing the perpetrator, the courts removed the victims. Girls who ran away were put on probation, and if they ran away again, they ended up in GRF.

These were tough girls. They got into fistfights, used foul language, and tried to survive on their own. These were angry girls. Karen wrote, "I taste sour lemon/and like black & blue/I smell fire." But all of these girls wanted attention and validation. They wanted boyfriends and female companions. They also wanted to be accepted by adults.

Most of all, they wanted to be loved. This crying out for affection permeated their poems; over and over, their call to "love me" seeped through. Janene wrote, "I once had a love and that love was strong!/But now it's done and over with 'cause/that person has gone and has forgotten about me."

Each year at GRF, the first round of poetry-writing workshops was in a classroom. For several months the whole class participated. Then the students revised their poems together on the board. After that, a pullout program was arranged for those students who wanted to write more poetry, and there was a nice little crowd outside. The yard was a grassy field, like any other field, only this one was surrounded with barbed wire. Still, being outside was somewhat freeing for writing.

Many students wrote about fantasies of hooking up with boys incarcerated across the way. But much of their work was also self-reflective, and it was obvious that they all needed a good dose of self-confidence. Denise wrote, "I would like to wake up/in the morning and see a/simple face with no pain in my eyes." The workshops were not designed to be poetry therapy, but they were, overwhelmingly, healing for the student.

One girl named Cynthia wrote poems all the time, not just during poetry workshops. She wrote with a passion that would save her life, if writing poems could do such a thing. She wrote about her life and the injustices she saw in the big world. She also wrote abuse, nature, love, and loss. She wrote, "I am bound between a lock and chain/Is my entire body entrapped/or is it only my heart?"

Cynthia was just thirteen and in for prostitution. She also drank. Poetry became a way to bond, and authorities encouraged a "VIP" (a volunteer who befriended a girl and visited, brought gifts, and sometimes took her on short excursions) relationship with her. But Cynthia had no VIP assigned to her; there was no one else in her life, no family member nearby, and she wanted an adult friend. "VIP" became part of the meaning of "visiting poet" for Cynthia.

During a few afternoons spent in the park, Cynthia confided about her life and shared more of her poetry. She was an AWOL risk and had even written letters to her VIP when she was on the run. Once, she had left for ten months before being brought back to GRF. But she never ran away during her VIP excursions.

When Cynthia's grandparents came to visit from Minnesota, they promised to take her to live with them, and Cynthia was excited about it. She wrote a letter to her VIP stating, "Once I get there I'll be taking up poetry, modern dancing, sunbathing, and swimming. It will probably be lots of fun, but I will miss many friends, especially you. My grandma said I could even have a dog."

Her prerelease visit with them was set for Easter. A good life with her grandparents, away from abuse, was now possible. But Cynthia went on her visit with her grandparents and ran away. Word got around the facility that she might be in Las Vegas, probably hooking. She was never brought back to GRF. Hopefully, somehow, her poetry saved her. This chapter is dedicated to her.

SAMPLE WRITING EXERCISES

1) Imagination: Objects That Take Us to Another Time and Place

Begin with the imagination, because that is the freeing element of poetry. Talk with students about how they can leave the facility and go anywhere they want in their imaginations. It can be a place where they'd like to go or a place that doesn't even exist, but everything they want is there. This is the place of their dreams free from prison walls and free from abuse.

Then present them with a bag of objects—all kinds of things, like seashells, stones, earrings, cloth, clover, grass, cotton, coral, clay, ribbons, rubber bands, apples—basically anything small that you can find in your house or yard. Some have smells and some have sounds. Put enough objects in the bag for each person to choose three.

Walk around the room and have the students reach into the bag and pick one object. Then circle again and again, at least three times. The students should concentrate on them one at a time, then choose the one that can represent something in their lives. Ask them to close their eyes and imagine where they are and what their surroundings look like. Ask, "What colors are there? What people are there? What details do you see? What sounds do you hear? How do you feel?"

At this point, they have transformed the object into a memory and the memory into a place and a specific time in their lives. Then read model poems that call up memories of times and places.

"I Ask My Mother to Sing," by Li-Young Lee

She begins, and my grandmother joins her.
Mother and daughter sing like young girls.
If my father were alive, he would play
his accordion and swing like a boat.

I've never been in Peking, or the Summer Palace,
nor stood on the great Stone Boat to watch
the rain begin on Kuen Ming Lake, the picnickers
running away in the grass.

But I love to hear it sung:
how the waterlilies fill with rain until
they overturn, spilling water into water,
then rock back, and fill with more.

Both women have begun to cry.
But neither stops her song.

Talk about the places in China the mother and grandmother sing about in this poem. The speaker has only heard about them; he's never been there. But the emotion comes through the poem when the mother and grandmother sing. They miss their old country and the speaker's father, who would play his accordion, if he were alive. Ask the students what object they think could have brought on this memory, such as a grape for a picnic. Then read another model poem of place.

"Islamorada," by Richard Blanco

Nets like cobwebs to the sea then he speaks
to the other sardine fishermen on the pier.
I lean like a sail to capture his voice, fill
with the wind from a distant 1040's Cuba.

Nets open and wet the pier, we gather
the silvery spill of bodies, through our hands
into buckets where they quiver for a while
then die above the lapping of waves.

The day ebbs into dusk, the sand thickens,
we fold the nets under the early stars,
then retreat from the sea as the tide turns,
our hands full, our mouths empty.

Islamorada means "purple island" and is located in the Florida Keys. The poet also references Cuba in the distance. This is a poem of place, describing the island where fishermen open their nets on the pier. A small piece of netting or anything from the sea could have inspired the poem.

Ask the students to write a poem related to their object, to associate it with a time and place, to describe where they are, what is happening around them, and how they feel. They can use their imaginations to fill in missing details. Another option is to make up a place where they'd like to go and put in people they'd like to have there. They can have anything they want happen to them.

Here's a poem by a student that takes the reader to a stormy sea. The mood is unsettling, and the poem can evoke fear, anger, or sadness, but it ends on a hopeful note.

"Storm's Image," by Cynthia, eighth grade

The wind, sounding like
a sea maiden crying for
her shipwrecked mate,
a screech in the breeze,
a howl speaking of death . . .
She weeps as her love gets thrown
against the rocks,
the waves crashing into each other.

Clouds, a sign of death
in the shape of black hearts,
form in the sky.
The devil, in the shape of a dove,
flies swiftly through the air.

Fear not my friends;
these things cannot harm you.
They want to be your friends
if you allow them.

2) Five Senses: Noticing Details, Using Senses—A Walk Around the Field

Ask the students to imagine what it would be like to live without being able to see where they are going, hear a conversation on the phone—the voice of someone they love—smell the flowers outside, feel a hug, or taste pizza and French fries. Wow, what a dull life that would be!

Then tell them to apply it to poetry. Say, "Tell me what a pine tree smells like at Christmas" or "what a bunny's fur feels like." Several students will chime in with examples. Nature is all around them, even here, on prison grounds. Go outside to the field where they play sports and sit in a circle while reading model poems about going out into fields. The first model poem has no title.

by Jalal ad-Din Muhammad Balkhi ("Rumi"), translated by Coleman Barks

Come to the orchard in spring.
There is light and wine and sweethearts
    in the pomegranate flowers.

If you do not come, these do not matter.
If you do come, these do not matter.

Tell the students that Rumi came from Persia, an area that is now part of Iran and part of Turkey, and he wrote poems eight hundred years ago in a language called Farsi. This poem is very sparse but has a lot of meaning; it's a love poem. The speaker will love the beloved no matter what. Also talk about how he names the kind of flowers, "pomegranates," and how he uses the senses of smell and sight. The next model poem uses four of the five senses.

"War Dog," by Elijah Imlay
    in Memory of Wayne Geivet

Take War Dog with you to patrol
the ammo dump, says Sergeant Geivet.
He's half-wild, never barks,
and he's got your back.

When he sniffs me, it's no surprise,
but when his panting fogs my glasses

Does Anybody Love Me?

I recall winter:
lenses steamed after a brisk walk,
storm doors and windows frosted over
and a welcome fire.
I smooth brindled fur matted with dust
and for a moment I'm home
with the neighbor's dog. Except
his tail is different, curled in a tight coil
common to Vietnamese breeds.
But he won't stay.
His eyes size me up quick and he's gone.
He pilfers the moment for a ham bone,
knocking a bucket over
as he turns a corner.
A yelping pack chases what it hears.

Here's a dog without tags.
Sure, he knows a few tricks,
but will he attack on command?
Built like a bull dog
but missing his eyeteeth
he gets fed by stray GI's.
Here dogs rove in packs
and are served in cafes.
Who's to say he won't run off.

After supper, rivals draw a crowd.
Spinning through dusk
they rip at underbelly and neck.
No way to hose them apart.
Sudden as nightfall, it's over,
a ritual without a death cry.
War Dog limps away.
When I walk beside him
we become friends,
and when I dress his deep gash
he licks my hidden wounds.

In this poem, the speaker is on guard duty in Vietnam. He goes into a field to patrol an ammunition dump and takes a wild dog with him. When he returns, the dog gets into a brawl with other dogs. The poet uses *smell* in the line "When he sniffs me, it's no surprise"; *touch* in the line "I smooth brindled fur matted with dust"; *sound* in the line "A yelping pack chases what it hears; and *sight* in the line "His eyes size me up quick and he's gone."

Before the students write, take them on a walk silently around the field, as if it were the first time they were there. Ask them to notice everything, not just the obvious, like a class doing sports, but also the unobvious, like a hole in the grass or a plant or the way the barbed wire looks. They can also notice what's in the sky. Ask them to breathe deeply and take in the smells, bend down and feel the grass—even roll in it if they want. By doing this, they can experience nature in a new way.

Then ask the students to write poems describing the experience they just had in a sensual way. Tell them to be observers of nature, but without using the abstract word "nature," to write about what's been out there all along, but that they hadn't noticed before—little details—and to use as many of their five senses as possible.

Here's a student poem with great visual details. The speaker sees things like she never has before, noticing details, a whole world inside a little hole where worms and grass live. She also uses similes referring to the hole she sees "as wide as my fist/and as deep as a golf hole."

"untitled," by Denise, ninth grade

> As I walk around this field
> that I thought I knew so well,
> I see a hole and I think,
> that wasn't there before.
> It wasn't very deep.
> It was about as wide as my fist
> and as deep as a golf hole.
> The sun left a crescent shadow on the side.
> The sides were crumbling down.
> And worms and grass
> making their way to the top.

3) Emotions: Feelings We Associate with Animals

Talk with students about expressing feelings in poetry and how they will want their poems to get an emotional response from the reader. Next, brainstorm emotions on the board. Then brainstorm types of animals. Choose one animal, like a tiger, and brainstorm words they associate with a tiger, such as swift, cunning, vicious, yellow/gold, big teeth, huge paws, and the like.

Take it one step further and choose a few of those words, like "cunning," and ask, "How is a tiger cunning? What does it do that makes it cunning?" "A tiger's like a detective," someone might say. Ask why. And the answer you might get is that it is always searching for something.

Take another word like "vicious" and discuss how the tiger hunts and kills its prey.

Then ask them to think about the tiger some more. Ask, "What does the tiger feel inside?" Tell them to try to climb inside and be the tiger and imagine its life. Then read a model poem that's about a tiger, but the word "tiger" is spelled differently.

"The Tyger," by William Blake

Tyger! Tyger! burning bright
In the forests of the night,
What immortal hand or eye
Could frame thy fearful symmetry?

In what distant deeps or skies
Burnt the fire of thine eyes?
On what wings dare he aspire?
What the hand dare seize the fire?

And what shoulder, and what art,
Could twist the sinews of thy heart?
And when thy heart began to beat,
What dread hand? and what dread feet?

What the hammer? what the chain?
In what furnace was thy brain?
What the anvil? what dread grasp
Dare its deadly terrors clasp?

When the stars threw down their spears,
And watered heaven with their tears,
Did he smile his work to see?
Did he who made the lamb make thee?

Tyger! Tyger! burning bright
In the forests of the night,
What immortal hand or eye,
Dare frame thy fearful symmetry?

This poem was written by the famous English poet, William Blake, in 1793, and therefore has rhyme, meter, and formal language. It's one of his most famous poems. William Blake questions who could make such a fearful, awesome animal. Then read another model poem.

"I Almost Didn't See," by Bruce Weigl

The toad was trapped; the drain was overflowed
from flooded downspouts in a summer storm.

>   He was a young and handsome toad, still lean from tadpole days,
> so I wanted to reach down
>   to lift him from the whirlpool he struggled
> to survive, but I wavered there.
>
> I'd come outside to watch the storm roll in its black and roiled clouds,
>   the rain we needed, rare as peace.
> He had to learn how not to die himself.
>   He didn't drown; I didn't reach to pull him out.

Talk about the worth of toads and how people see them without really paying attention to them. Here, the speaker notices the toad and wants to save him. But the speaker knows that the toad "had to learn how not to die himself." In other words, he had to save himself. This might make the students think about their future outside of the walls that entrap them and give them hope that they can also save themselves.

Ask them to choose an animal and write a poem describing what it looks like, how it behaves, and how it might feel. They can use any setting they want. It doesn't have to be a wild animal; it can also be a pet. What's important is that their feelings come through the poem without their stating them outright.

Here's a student poem that is a wonderful description of a wild panther, moving quickly through the jungle on a hot summer day. The student uses a great simile: "As silent as death." She really gets inside that panther and captures his essence. She also describes what he looks like, how he behaves, and what he feels, "hoping not to convey the murder/that maddens his mind."

"Black Panther," by Jan, tenth grade

Rays beating down from the hot summer sun
glisten on the panther's black coat.
You can see the despise from the gleam
in his eyes, that reveals nothing
but mystery and apathy.

As silent as death
he roams the jungle floor,
with the swiftness and ease
of a hot summer breeze.
While stalking his prey he looks down
in an eerie, hell-evil way,
hoping not to convey the murder
that maddens his mind.

More smooth than velvet and blacker than sun
the panther's fine coat holds all this within.

4) Imagery, Simile, and Metaphor: Go Inside a Picture of a Famous Star

Talk about how imagery comes right out of the word "imagination" and people use their imaginations to create images. Sometimes people use metaphors or similes in poems, which create instant images and light up the picture with special effects. Ask the students to come up with some simile examples: "The stars are like glitter in my eyes," "the air is as cold as fruit inside the fridge," or "the dew is wet like my tongue."

Then make the similes into metaphors, by taking away "like" or "as": "The stars *are* glitter in my eyes," "the air *is* cold fruit inside the fridge," or "the dew *is* a wet tongue." They don't have to make sense. That's why it's called figurative language. Tell them that today they'll be painting portraits or creating "word photos" of movie stars, inside and out.

Read the model poems. The first one is by a poet who was writing during the Romantic Period, the early 1800s in England, so it is not in free verse; it has meter and rhyme. And it perfectly captures the beauty and eloquence of a woman of stature.

"She Walks in Beauty," by George Gordon, Lord Byron

She walks in beauty, like the night
   Of cloudless climes and starry skies;
And all that's best of dark and bright
   Meet in her aspect and her eyes:
Thus mellow'd to that tender light
   Which heaven to gaudy day denies.

One shade the more, one ray the less,
   Had half impair'd the nameless grace
Which waves in every raven tress,
   Or softly lightens o'er her face;
Where thoughts serenely sweet express
   How pure, how dear their dwelling-place.

And on that cheek, and o'er that brow,
   So soft, so calm, yet eloquent,
The smiles that win, the tints that glow,
   But tell of days in goodness spent,
A mind at peace with all below,
   A heart whose love is innocent!

The poem begins with a simile: "She walks in beauty, like the night." The speaker is overwhelmed by this beauty. You can see it in lines like, "And on that cheek, and o'er that brow/So soft, so calm, yet eloquent/The smiles that win, the tints that glow" and in the last lines, where the speaker gets inside of the woman and tries to imagine how she might feel: "A mind at peace with all below/A heart whose love is innocent!"

The next model poem describes the singer/actress Cher. Since it's very long, only read the first third of the poem.

from "Cher," by Dorianne Laux

> I wanted to be Cher, tall
> as a glass of iced tea,
> her bony shoulders draped
> with a curtain of dark hair
> that plunged straight down,
> the cut tips brushing
> her nonexistent butt.
> I wanted to wear a lantern
> for a hat, a cabbage, a piñata
> and walk in thigh-high boots
> with six-inch heels that buttoned
> up the back. I wanted her
> rouged cheek bones and her
> throaty panache, her voice
> of gravel and clover, the hokum
> of her clothes: black fishnet
> and pink pom-poms, frilled
> halter tops, fringed bells
> and her thin strip of waist
> with the bullet-hole navel.
> Cher standing with her skinny arm
> slung around Sonny's thick neck,
> posing in front of the Eiffel Tower,
> The Leaning Tower of Pisa,
> The Great Wall of China,
> the Crumbling Pyramids, smiling
> for the camera with her crooked
> teeth, hit-and-miss beauty, the sun
> bouncing off the bump on her nose.

Point out the details in the portrait that the poet creates of Cher, beginning with the simile, "tall/as a glass of iced tea." The images allow the reader to easily imagine the picture of this tall woman with long, dark hair and crooked teeth. He or she can see what Cher is wearing and imagine her posing for pictures.

Then pass out pictures from popular teen magazines of movie stars the students recognize. Tell them to choose a picture of someone who speaks to them. Once they have their pictures, ask them to get inside and become those people for a moment, to observe what they look like, what they like to wear, what their favorite colors are, and so forth.

Then ask the students to look into their chosen stars' eyes and imagine their lives. The students only know them as famous movie stars, but in their personal lives they might not always be smiling. They might have problems with marriage or kids; on the other hand, they might have very happy lives.

The assignment is to write a poem describing the person in the chosen picture, using strong imagery with some metaphors and/or similes, if desired. The description should be physical, but the students should also imagine the people's lives and how happy or sad they are, based on the look on their faces and in their eyes and not on what the students might have read about the stars.

Here is a poem by a student who describes "Hollywood Stars"—what these women's lives are like walking the streets in Hollywood. They are described as wearing "a costume of high heels/and rabbit coats." The mood of the poem is somber. These are not happy women, and they aren't really stars at all.

"Hollywood Stars," by Cynthia, eighth grade

As they silently walk the streets at night,
Cars honk,
Police play as spies.
Who are these lovely ladies of the night?
Dressed so seductively, each wearing
a costume of high heels
and rabbit coats.
They play their role every night.
Are they the leading star or will they ever
make it that far?
Who will ever know?
Their mother, father or baby sister and brother?
What will happen when they're too old for their role?
Will they be left alone in the cold,
as their producer walks around in gold?
Why does this happen to each lady of the dark?
Why can't they change?
    Their lives made right.
        Why must they walk alone?
            In the silence of the night.

Part II: Colston Youth Center

Trapped like a tree raccoon
No place to run . . .
Trapped in a cold cubicle on a bed of concrete
wishing I was free

—Sean, tenth grade

"The Boy Who Eats Worms," by Shelley Savren

The sun bruises the darkness . . .
A scrap of wind falls . . .
The hunger grows worse each day . . .
An ax in the bois d'arc tree . . .

—Jerome, ninth grade

The sun bruises the darkness
and the blood inside this boy
in my poetry class at Juvie.
So he sets stuff on fire and uses drugs,
but here's a kid whose parents hung him
like a coat in the closet for hours
before he could walk.

A scrap of wind falls
and he appears with a poem
translated from a language he invented
complete with alphabet and sound
though he never speaks it,
only writes it in his room at lockdown
when he isn't eating worms
dug up by kids who dare him.

The hunger grows worse each day
and when he doesn't show
the teacher says he shaved his eyebrows
for a joke, gashed his arm
to watch blood spurt psychedelic purple
across the floor and walls.

An ax in the bois d'arc tree—
he is both ax and tree
but no one deals with a boy like that.
Guards refuse to clean the blood
and the county ships him
to a placement home up north.

He's now a Buddhist, I'm told,
uses magic and makes stuff disappear,
like he's disappeared so many times.

After the move from San Diego to Ventura, California, in 1992, the goal was to continue working with incarcerated youth, so over a ten-year period, several short poetry-writing workshop sessions took place at Frank A. Colston Youth Center. It was a lockdown co-ed facility, but the vast majority of those incarcerated were boys.

The few girls who were there were tough on the outside. They were mainly gang members and frequently had babies at home, but they also slept with Teddy bears and cried in their cells at night. Once a staff member called at night requesting that the visiting poet come sit with one of the girls. She was in the community room, scared to return to her cell and wanting to spend the night reading the poems she'd written.

The boys ranged from ages twelve to eighteen, but most were high school age. Many were gangbangers and participated in criminal activities, such as burglary, car theft, stabbings, drive-by shootings, and other violent crimes; some were in for drug or alcohol abuse, parole violations, or truancy. Their average stay was three months to a year. However, many times they couldn't seem to stay out of trouble and returned again and again. A tenth grader, Andy, wrote:

I am a river flowing
between these cold walls
and if I don't change my direction,
I will cut a deeper wall that I must face.
Deeper into the system I flow
unable to change my ways.

Most of the students came from harsh backgrounds where they were victims of abuse, poverty, or neglect. It was common for them to have alcoholic or drug abuser parents and not unusual to have one parent in prison. When it was time for them to be released, they were often sent to placement homes or back to foster care. Frequently, they had no positive adult role models at home and often had no one to encourage them in school or to just listen to them or to simply love them.

Many of the students were behind in credits in school; some were academic underachievers, and several of them had learning disabilities. But some were brilliant writers and took to poetry easily. The classes were very structured. The students all wore the required white T-shirts and jeans, and they were given course credit for participating. So unlike at the GRF, there were lots of rules to follow. A visiting poet coming in was just another adult who had authority in their lives, and that image had to be quickly dispelled.

Mutual respect had to be established right away. It was important to speak their language, using expressions like, "Write about your homies; write about cruising your 'hood." And they did. Ben wrote, "My mom just let me know that my homie passed away." Andy wrote of his arrest: "I had no chance to throw my knife or my baggies."

When conducting workshops for incarcerated youths, showing mutual respect also means not denigrating their gangs. Gangs are their friends, their families. They need to know that there is nothing wrong with hanging out with friends; it's *the activities* that they choose to participate in that are bad. But that doesn't mean that they can't write about them. In fact, they should be encouraged to write about their gangs, which helps to establish trust.

However, in most of these facilities students are not allowed to *glorify* gang activities in poems, and they can't use colors that represent their gangs. So that they don't get into trouble and don't have to censor what they write, encourage them to write *those* poems in their cells and not during class. Many of them find that to be a great reason to keep writing on their own, which of course, is the goal.

These students are a captive audience, but they still need to get "turned on" to poetry. Considering the fact that they are subject to the same peer pressure as all teens, writing poetry is not the coolest thing to do. That notion has to be changed. The process needs to enable them to reach inside, find their feelings, and express them in poems. They need to trust the process and the visiting poet, so they can tell their stories and write about their lives. They need to find poetry to be empowering, a tool for survival, an alternative to destructive activities, a vehicle for self-acceptance, and a way to change who they are.

The workshops at Colston consisted of three or four sessions each time, and every time there was a new workshop series, there were new students. The teachers at Colston School were excellent in their jobs, and they completely supported the poetry-writing program. In fact, they even brought some students, along with an officer from the facility, to the neighboring Oxnard College to meet the college students and participate in a poetry reading arranged by the visiting poet.

The good news was that the students really liked writing. One interesting thing was that they loved getting stickers on their poems. Stickers were put on little kids' poems, but these *big* kids seriously loved getting them. They also genuinely liked to read their poems aloud to the class, not just because they got credit for reading them, but because they loved getting validation from other students, from their teacher, and from the visiting poet.

And they were vulnerable, often putting aside that tough veneer and showing their concern about their families. Carlos wrote, "I heard sounds of a gun/

Blood was everywhere and all I could think about/was what my mom was going to say." Some of them revealed their fears—not fears of other gangs, but fears from their childhood. Sean wrote:

> Microscopic nightmares linger in the corners and cracks
> where decades of dirt and decay have nestled.
> Childhood fears, teeth, claws, bones.
> Don't go in the cellar.

Some of them surprised themselves. A hard-core gang member read a poem he wrote about his grandma, broke down crying, and had to leave the room (with permission and with the aide). Several wrote love poems to their girlfriends.

One boy, Jerome, had a miserable background of abuse, was taken away by the court when he was very young, and was living with adoptive parents. He only came to a couple of poetry-writing workshops. But he showed up one day with a poem he wrote, saying that he created a new language for it and then translated it into English. The poem was so powerful that it was published in the CPITS statewide anthology (and is used as a model student poem for Exercise 3). For him, poetry was a passion, a friend, a place to crawl inside and imagine another world.

One day, when he didn't show up, the teacher said that he had cut himself, and blood was all over his cell. Eventually, he was released into placement, and the teacher said that he was doing well. Unfortunately that didn't last. Like many of those kids, Jerome found that life on the streets was tough; after he turned eighteen, he wound up in prison. Whatever happened to him, one can only hope that he kept writing.

SAMPLE WRITING EXERCISES

1) Imagination: Guided Fantasy

For today's lesson, tell the students that they are going to use their imaginations and go on a guided fantasy journey. Explain that they will be asked questions that they are to answer in their minds, not out loud. Then begin the following, slowly:

> *Close your eyes; let your body relax; allow your breath to fall evenly. You are about to take a journey, and you will answer the questions in your mind.*
>
> *This journey will take you far away to a safe place. Choose your method of travel: skateboard, surfboard, roller blades, hot air balloon, jet skis, airplane, cloud, rocket—you decide how you will get there.*

Have your vehicle ready. And now, one last time, visualize this room, this place. Dump everything you hate into it—algebra, history, people you don't like, anything you don't want in your life.

Now get ready to ride . . . and poof! The room is gone and you are flying free. Notice your surroundings as you travel—the colors, the smells, the sounds, the tastes in the air. Describe the terrain. Are you in a forest? An ocean? A desert? On a mountain? Reach out and touch the world and hold it in your hand as you land in a special place.

This is the place you've dreamed of. You are there, and it is everything you've wanted. Create this place of your dreams. What does it look like? What things are there? Make it full of hope.

Now bring in everyone who means something special to you—your friends, your family, your dog or another pet. Do something fun with them. Take a picture of the moment when you are the happiest and most fulfilled.

Now hold that picture close to you. Press it into your heart. Memorize it. Fill your pockets with this place, these people, this memory, and take it with you.

Now get back on your vehicle. You are traveling, and you must return, but not to the place you left. That place is gone. In its place is something new. It's a place where you can be more hopeful. Remember what fills your pockets.

Now breathe deeply and open your eyes.

At this point, go through various parts of their journey and ask them what their vehicle was, where they landed, what it looked like, and who was there. Search for details created in their imaginations. Then read model poems.

"The Painter," by Amy Uyematsu
     after Pissarro
morning
When gray resolves
     into its pale
          yellow gaze
river
makes no sound
     even this boat
          in the silent mist
fog
the hidden hours
     a footless man
          floats toward me

Here, the speaker finds herself in a boat floating along a river. It's foggy, and she sees "a footless man" floating toward her, ending the poem in mystery. Then read another model poem that also takes place in the fog.

"Place of Mind," by Richard Blanco

Mist haunts the city, tears of rain fall
from the awnings and window ledges.
The search for myself begins an echo
drifting away the moment I arrive.

From the awnings the window ledges
follow the rain flowing down the streets.
The moment I arrive, I drift away:
Why am I always imagining the sea?

Follow the rain flowing down the streets
vanishing into the mouths of gutters.
Why am I always imagining the sea?
A breath, a wave—a breath, a wave.

Vanishing into the mouths of gutters,
rain becomes lake, river, ocean again.
A breath, a wave—a breath, a wave
always beginning, yet always ending.

Rain becomes lake, river, ocean, again
mist haunts the city, tears of rain fall.
Always ending, yet always beginning,
the search for myself ends in echo.

    This poem shows a person searching for himself as the rain transforms into a lake, a river, and an ocean. Point out that the poem is a pantoum, written in quatrains (four lines to a stanza), in which the second and fourth lines are repeated as the first and third lines of the following stanza.
    Ask the students to write a poem about any part of their journey they want. It can be about taking a ride on a skateboard or describing the place where they landed with all its smells, sights, and sounds, or the time they spent with their special friend. They can also journey to places of mystery as in the model poems and continue to use their imagination and add more details to their poem.
    Here's a student poem that describes the place of his dreams in great detail. It uses strong diction, like "lumbering" and "cracking." Point out the alliteration, the repetition of consonant sounds in "painting patterns . . ." and "clay cliff . . ." and mention that they'll be learning alliteration in a future lesson. The ending is also symbolic. The clearing in the natural setting is compared to the clearing in the speaker's heart.

"A Special Clearing," by Travis, eleventh grade

As I'm lumbering through brush
spewed trails cracking brush and sticks as a bear.

When I break through the brush I hit
a clearing, a beautiful clearing.

There's a babbling brook asking for a listening friend.
As the rocks slowly tumble down
a rocky clay cliff shaping into a living thing
as it heaves it cracks in the middle to show me
wonders never seen.

On the old willow a spider plays
with diamond thread painting patterns throughout
the tree for the morning breeze.

When midday hits with a high snowy mountain breeze
the diamond thread turns to
a bright golden hue while the willow stretches
its hand like branches over the brook
to shade all. The bugs are buzzing like a nest of bees
flying around in the breeze.

At early night the fog lifts off the lake
as a steam lifts off a tub of hot water.
The fog raises the crests of all living things
like a hesitant lover craving a touch.
This is my clearing in my heart.

2) Emotions: Poems of Loss

Talk about the importance of expressing feelings in poems and how to effectively do that. Then talk about loss. Everyone has lost something, and not all loss is a bad thing. For example, everyone has lost teeth or a pencil. It's great for most people when they lose weight. Sometimes people lose "baggage" that they don't need and want to let go of, friends who have betrayed them in some way, and so on. Of course, there's also painful loss. A dog dies, or worse, a grandparent dies. Or the family moves away, and they lose a friend.

Read the model poems to the students. The first one enumerates all kinds of things and people that the speaker has lost and serves as a great brainstorm for the students.

"The Lost Things," by Jack Grapes

I lost my hiking boots.
And my green sleeping bag.
Maybe someone stole them.
Anyway, they're gone.

So is my copy of
Hear Us O Lord
From Heaven
Thy Dwelling Place
by Malcolm Lowry.
So are some other books.
Daniele left my red baseball cap
with the silver wings of mercury
in the bathroom at Barbera's Pizza Parlor.
And I can't find my favorite pair of scissors
either, not to mention
my Bluit camping stove
and large cooking pot.
I loaned them to Karen Kaplowitz
coming out of the Cucamonga Wilderness
and she still has them.
She's a lawyer.
Now my mail isn't coming.
Someone put in a change of address form
and the post office
has been forwarding my mail
to the Graduate Department of English
at the University of Pittsburgh.
This is true.
"Why am I losing these things,"
I keep asking.
I keep asking this.
Out loud.
I'm driving Lori crazy.
"Something strange is going on here,"
I yell.
It's getting hard to concentrate on anything
for very long.
"Where are my boots," I whine
in the middle of a movie.
My favorite hiking boots.
It's very distressing.
Someone has my sleeping bag right now
and they're hurting it.
Someone's grimy hands are pulling apart
Hear Us O Lord From Heaven Thy Dwelling Place
and they don't even care about the underlines
or the notes I've made in the margins.
I'm not going to let it get to me.

The red hat, with the silver wings of mercury,
I plan to get back if it's the last thing I do.
I'll keep a look out
and someday whoever took it
will be wearing it in the May Co.
thinking I've forgotten all about it.
But I haven't.
I'll see it.
And I'll get it back.
I'll get all my things back.
My Bluit camping stove
and my large cooking pot.
And my mail, all my mail.
My sleeping bag.
My boots.
My broken-in hiking boots.
I've missed you all so much.
So very much.
The lost things are coming back.
It's all coming back to me.
And I need to feel that I deserve this.
I need to learn
how to open my arms
and take them in,
as I would myself,
lost
these many
many
years.

Talk about the humor in this poem, in the tone, the attitude that the author brings to it. It could be very upsetting to lose all those things, but the way the poet writes it makes the reader laugh. The next model poem, by an Israeli poet, talks about a love lost.

"I Passed a House," by Yehuda Amichai, translated by Glenda Abramson and Tudor Parfitt

I passed a house where I once lived:
A man and a woman are still together in the whispers.
Many years have passed with the silent buzz
of the staircase bulbs—on, off, on.

The keyholes are like small delicate wounds
through which all the blood has oozed out
and inside people are pale as death.

I want to stand once more as in my
first love, leaning on the doorpost
embracing you all night long, standing.
When we left at early dusk the house
started to crumble and collapse
and since then the town
and since then the whole world.

I want once more to have this longing
until dark-red burn marks show on the skin.

I want once more to be written
in the book of life, to be written
anew each day
until the writing hand hurts.

Ask the students to write a poem about loss that expresses their feelings without stating them, by re-creating an experience or describing what happened that made the speaker feel a certain way. The poem can be humorous, like Jack Grapes' poem, or serious, like Yehuda Amichai's poem.

Here's a student poem about death, the ultimate loss. There is sadness in the poem, but the poet didn't say he was sad; he simply described what happened and his relationship to the loss. There is wonderful language, such as the use of the adjective "swift" as a past tense verb in "and quickly swifted him up" and the simile, "My mom came storming in/like a bull." There is also the great image of "the naked cold wind."

"I Love You Brother," by Vincent, ninth grade

My brother died at age 10.
The breath left his lungs.
I tried to help him
but he vanished into the wind.
His soul left his body.
My mom came storming in
like a bull
and quickly swifted him up
and rushed him to the hospital.
It was later that day
when he didn't make it.
I'll always love him
through the naked cold wind.
Forever and ever
I will remember that day
when my twin brother vanished
and went his own way.

3) Imagery and Persona: Teen Image

Talk about imagery and how people use their imaginations to create images. Then suggest that there is another type of image, the face that people present to the world. Introduce the term "persona." It's a mask people hide behind when presenting themselves. They can also pretend they are someone else and write in first person from that point of view, or they can write from their own point of view as a child.

Everyone has a different mask or persona that she or he uses for different people. People behave differently, for example, around their grandmothers than they do around their homies. They use a different language.

Also, how they dress and how they wear their hair present an impression to the world. For example, in the late sixties, hippies grew their hair long, wore bell-bottom jeans, flashed peace signs, and played guitars in the streets. Nowadays lots of young people have piercings and tattoos and wear styles different from those of their parents' generation.

Then read some model poems. The first one presents the persona of a scared man in prison, something some of the students can relate to.

"Like an Animal," by Jimmy Santiago Baca

Behind the smooth texture
Of my eyes, way inside me,
A part of me has died:
I move my bloody fingernails
Across it, hard as a blackboard,
Run my fingers along it,
The chalk white scars
That say I AM SCARED,
Scared of what might become
Of me, the real me,
Behind these prison walls.

Talk about the image of bloody fingernails and "the smooth texture/Of my eyes. . . ." And talk about the person's fear of becoming someone the person doesn't want to be. Then read a poem that presents the persona of a young girl.

"The Leaving," by Brigit Pegeen Kelly

My father said I could not do it,
but all night I picked the peaches.
The orchard was still, the canals ran steadily.
I was a girl then, my chest its own walled garden.
How many ladders to gather an orchard?

I had only one and a long patience with lit hands
and the looking of the stars which moved right through me
the way the water moved through the canals with a voice
that seemed to speak of this moonless gathering
and those who had gathered before me.
I put the peaches in the pond's cold water,
all night up the ladder and down, all night my hands
twisting fruit as if I were entering a thousand doors,
all night my back a straight road to the sky.
And then out of its own goodness, out
of the far fields of the stars, the morning came,
and inside me was the stillness a bell possesses
just after it has been rung, before the metal
begins to long again for the clapper's stroke.
The light came over the orchard.
The canals were silver and then were not.
and the pond was—I could see as I laid
the last peach in the water—full of fish and eyes.

Here is a young person taking on a challenge that her father didn't think she could handle. Most young people can relate to that. Point out the wonderful imagery, "my chest its own walled garden," "canals with a voice/that seemed to speak of moonless gathering," "entering a thousand doors," and "before the metal/begins to long again for the clapper's stroke." The images add pictures to the story of a girl picking peaches, making the atmosphere come alive. Through these pictures, the reader can see the persona of a girl steadfast in her task of picking peaches.

For this writing assignment, ask the students to focus on imagery. They can write a persona poem if they like, stepping into someone else's life and becoming them, or they can write in their own persona as a child or in an imaginary persona. Or they can just write a poem with lots of imagery where they hide behind a mask, not revealing who they really are. They can also use the face or persona of a type of person, such as a popular girl or guy who shows one side of herself or himself, but not the hurt, vulnerable side.

Here is a poem by a student written in the persona of an old man. The poem is loaded with images—"The sun bruises the darkness" and "A scrap of wind falls from the sky"—and with many similes—"like a pebble thrown by a careless young boy," "like a duck shot by a hunter over a pond in spring," "like old people in the attic," "like a puppy runs to a long-gone master," "like a grain of sand in an eye," "like a fan with its power cut off," and "like seaweed in a current." The mood is one of hopelessness, but it's powerfully rendered with images of the old man.

"The Grace of a Falling Angel," by Jerome, ninth grade

All alone
on a rock in an endless sea
like a pebble thrown by a careless young boy.
Here I sit on my beach.
My feet turn pink with cold
as icy water rushes to meet them.

It is sunset.
The sun bruises the darkness
in its dying struggle
for domination of the sky.
A scrap of wind falls from the sky
to ruffle and frolic in my hair.
A seagull drops
from the clouds to the sea
like a duck shot by a hunter over a pond in spring.

The hunger grows worse each day
but I still have nothing to feed it.
I will die out here,
but I sit on the beach
and think back on my life
like old people in the attic
watching an old film
of weddings and days at the park.
It has been a full life.

The old man stands
and walks toward the sea.
The sea rushes to meet him
like a puppy runs to a long-gone master.
The freezing water slaps the old man
with all its fury
but cannot match the old man's resolve.

Still he moves on.
An ax in the bois d'arc tree.
He moves on.
He can walk no longer,
now he must swim.
The sea does its best
to flush him out
like a grain of sand in an eye.

The water eases and turns
into sand dunes of water.
He swims on,

forgetting the sea,
forgetting the cold.
He thinks of his boyhood,
his first lover, his wedding.
His last words before the darkness takes him:
"It has been a good life."

His arms and legs stop paddling
like a fan with its power cut off.
His carcass floats down
with the grace of a falling angel.

His hair is like seaweed in a current.
This is the old man's funeral.
The fish are his only mourners.

4) Rhythm and Alliteration: Rap Poems

Emphasize that rhythm is an essential element of poetry. You can hear the beat, feel the beat, move to it, and sometimes snap your fingers to it. Sounds are also important when creating rhythm, and using alliteration, the repetition of consonant sounds, adds to the music of a poem. Then talk about rap music. They can all relate to it. It's a form of poetry, too, that uses rhyme. Good rap poems, like all poems, are carefully rendered with words that have meaning.

Then read model poems. Begin with one that isn't intended to be a rap poem; but, because of its rhythm, it sounds like a rap poem when you read it out loud. It's also one that the students can relate to, because it's about baseball, and guess what? They can write poems about sports!

"Analysis of Baseball," by May Swenson

It's about
the ball,
the bat,
and the mitt.
Ball hits
bat, or it
hits mitt.
Bat doesn't
hit ball, bat
meets it.
Ball bounces
off bat, flies
air, or thuds
ground (dud)
or it
fits mitt.

Bat waits
for ball
to mate.
Ball hates
to take bat's
bait. Ball
flirts, bat's
late, don't
keep the date.
Ball goes in
(thwack) to mitt,
and goes out
(thwack) back
to mitt.

Ball fits
mitt, but
not all
the time.
Sometimes
ball gets hit
(pow) when bat
meets it,
and sails
to a place
where mitt
has to quit
in disgrace.
That's about
the bases
loaded,
about 40,000
fans exploded.

It's about
the ball,
the bat,
the mitt,
the bases
and the fans.
It's done
on a diamond,
and for fun.
It's about
home, and it's
about run.

Talk about all the sounds and repetitions used in this poem and how rhyme is used effectively. The poet also uses alliteration in the lines, "Ball bounces/off bat . . . ," repeating the consonant B. In fact, that B sound is repeated throughout the poem, as in the lines, "Ball hates/to take bat's/bait. . . ."

The next model poem *is* rap. The poem gives a history of where the speaker lived and a strong image of who he is.

**"A Poem for Myself
(or Blues for a Mississippi Black Boy)," by Etheridge Knight**

I was born in Mississippi;
I walked barefooted thru the mud.
Born black in Mississippi,
Walked barefooted thru the mud.
But, when I reached the age of twelve
I left that place for good.
My daddy he chopped cotton
And he drank his liquor straight.
Said my daddy chopped cotton
And he drank his liquor straight.
When I left that Sunday morning
He was leaning on the barnyard gate.
I left my momma standing
With the sun shining in her eyes.
Left her standing in the yard
With the sun shining in her eyes.
And I headed North
As straight as the Wild Goose Flies,
I been to Detroit & Chicago—
Been to New York city too.
I been to Detroit and Chicago
Been to New York city too.
Said I done strolled all those funky avenues
I'm still the same old black boy with the same old blues.
Going back to Mississippi
This time to stay for good
Going back to Mississippi
This time to stay for good—
Gonna be free in Mississippi
Or dead in the Mississippi mud.

Talk about the descriptions of the speaker and his father and the rhythm that the poet uses. There's repetition and rhyme, but there's no set meter or pattern to the poem. And it's rhythmical. It's a rap poem, but it's still free verse. The image of the young boy is strong and sets a tone of struggle and pride.

Then ask the students to write poems that have distinct rhythms to them. They can be rap poems, but caution them to worry about rhyming and to choose their words carefully. While some popular rap music is violent or oppressive, that's not the kind they should write. Another choice is to write poems that repeat words or phrases. Or they can just write poems with very short lines or very long lines.

Here's a poem by a student that sounds like rap. The music of this poem is powerful, and it's easy for readers to move to it in some way, nodding heads or snapping fingers. There's also alliteration in the words "couldn't comprehend." The tone is somewhat depressing because the speaker feels trapped, something they can all relate to.

"What Can I Do?" by LaQuinta, twelfth grade

An innocent child growing up in the wilderness
living in a world of terror, hatred, and bitterness.
My mind was spinning. I couldn't comprehend.
Sometimes I wished that my life would journey to the end.
I was so sick, but I was tired of being sick.
My life was hanging from the edge of a cliff.
I was living in a world that people thought was crazy,
uneducated little girls out having babies,
little boys were on the corner outside selling rock.
My mom used to ask me when will it ever stop,
but that was a question I just couldn't understand.
A youngster growing up in the ghetto already a grown man
surviving the game—that's what it's all about.
My mom went through pain keeping food in my family's house
But our great dream evaporated when Pops got a murder case,
life with no parole. Never again would I see his face.
My life is living in terror and a lot of suspense.
But I can't do nothing, when I'm living behind a fence.

Chapter Four

The Urgent Landscape
Writing Poetry on College Campuses

> *these words I write*
> *open their mouths wide*
> *screaming the most intimate secrets*
> *I am the only one here*
> *I am the listener*
> *I know beautiful secrets*
>
> —Krista, *from* "To My Book"

"Welcome This Graduation Day," by Shelley Savren

In the swirling gardens of childhood
your imaginations scooped up dreams,
and you rode them, leaping wildly
into laughing clouds and coloring
the grass a slushy blue. You could be
anyone. You could even fly.

Your visions blossomed like wheat
in steaming fields, like tiny sprouts
poking out of concrete cracks,
in classrooms where there's always
a window to wander through,
always an arm stretching in the distance.

And here you sit, rows
of tall faces, with serious lips
and questioning eyes. Which door
to step through? Which road is a circle
and which a labyrinth?
Which braids and which bends?

> Soon you will stand like ageless redwoods
> reaching, knowing there is more
> to risk in the urgent landscape,
> more books to bow your heads into, words
> and numbers to rearrange the page,
> more gravel to stomp through
> in your sturdy, crusted boots.
>
> Everything rooted grows. Every path
> has a purpose and a name.
> Every pulsing passion opens, like dew
> waking up a morning meadow,
> like the sound of summer breathing
> in the backyard. Even now,
> the sun drenches you with light,
> and drunk on whirling ideas
> you will become navigators
> in the boundless playground of thought.

After teaching a few poetry-writing classes at University of California, San Diego and Southwestern College in Chula Vista, California, creative writing classes became part of a full-time teaching load at Oxnard College in Ventura County, California, from 1992 to 2014. Even though the course was creative writing and consisted of four genres, about half the time was spent on poetry because it was often the most challenging genre for students. Sometimes students still needed to get excited about poetry, but enthusiasm was usually contagious. And there have been many success stories over the years.

At the college level, the role of "visiting poet" takes on a new meaning. There really isn't a visiting poet, just a professor—the sole teacher in charge—and writing poetry becomes serious stuff. The course needs to be rigorous. It's not just an easy elective. Students pay for the course and take it for credit. This means they have to buy books, turn in work, and get a grade. It's a whole other world when it comes to academia.

There are plenty of good creative writing texts out there, but often those books are very expensive for students. Many of them have a prescribed way of approaching poetry or teaching creative writing. But trade books can do the job very well. Bill Moyers's *The Language of Life: A Festival of Poets* (ISBN 0-385-48410-0) has a great selection of contemporary poetry, along with interviews by Moyers with the poets, who talk about their process of writing, how they came to writing, what poetry means to them, and what they are trying to say in the individual poems published in the book.

During the course, students choose a poet, make a five-minute oral presentation with information just from the book, and end by reading a poem. That way, they get to know one poet well. And they can see how poets have very different writing processes.

Another great book to use is Clive Matson's *Let the Crazy Child Write: Finding Your Creative Writing Voice* (ISBN 978-1-880032-35-0). The author approaches writing intuitively and has a lot of inspiration to give to students. Often, creative writing professors have published books of poetry of their own, and they can offer those titles as optional reading, as in *The Common Fire* (ISBN: 978-1-888996-96-8) and *The Wild Shine of Oranges* (978-1-893670-44-0). Poems in books like these can be used as models for exercises, along with poems by other poets appearing in *The Language of Life*.

To start the college course with a bang, have students watch the documentary DVD, *The Power of the Word: Dancing on the Edge of the Road*, produced by Films for the Humanities & Sciences, which features the great American poet Stanley Kunitz reading his poems and discussing poetry with the author/editor/interviewer/journalist Bill Moyers (also available on Vimeo.com). Kunitz presents great insights on writing poems—everything from the gestation process to revision—and what he says is inspiring. This sets the tone for the semester.

Then give the students a poetry packet, which includes all the handouts and writing exercises. Use the first handout, "Statement on Poetry," to open up a discussion.

STATEMENT ON POETRY

Poetry is the art of transforming the human spirit through words. It is an expression of innermost thoughts and feelings put into a lyrical or narrative form—an art form that utilizes the sensual, the experiential, and the imaginative, paying close attention to sounds, images, rhythm, and the line. Poetry expresses thoughts and emotions while revealing truths.

Poems do not exist in voids. They come from inspirations and are shaped from many elements in our world, inside and out. Although the words cannot be forced, poems can be elicited by providing inspiration, such as reading other poems, walking in nature, and witnessing or experiencing the traumas and joys of living. Some poems come as unexpected gifts, and the poet's job is to honor that inspiration and create whenever the muse arrives. A poet must be fully open to the universe sensually and be ready to translate perceptions into words at any time. This is the poet's most vital task.

Words are the tools of poetry. A poet's job is to manipulate language. Often it is also necessary to alter information for the sake of the poem. While the poet must be true to the essence of the experience, she or he is not bound to the truth of the facts. His or her job is that of a craftsperson, and once the inspiration has settled in, a fitting language must be found. The poet often bursts out the initial piece, then piles on more layers while simultaneously carving away useless language—much like the sculptor piles on and shaves away clay on her or his working model.

The poet's ear is essential for finding her or his voice. The poet must read the poem aloud and listen to the sounds and rhythms that form this piece of art. He or she must intuit where the line starts and stops, taking into account where the emphasis should fall and whether or not a phrase should stop or continue into the next line. The form of a poem must always be a revelation, rather than a dictator of the content, in free verse. However, the two work together in crafting a poem.

The more detailed and the less abstract a poem is, the more universal it will become. In order to move people to a higher plane of thought or emotion, a poem must give the reader something concrete to relate to. Thus, poems that recreate experiences, describe details of a situation, and create motion pictures will be received with impact and understanding on the part of the reader.

Poems should be clear and layered with meaning. Poems that narrow an experience or disguise it in abstractions often lack depth and will be confusing and uninteresting to the reader. This is not to say that imagery is not essential to poetry. Fresh, clear images add music to the lyrics and vision to the words and create a higher order of language, which differentiates poetry from prose. This may include metaphor, simile, and other figurative forms of speech.

Revision is an essential part of crafting poetry. The process of creating a poem is essentially twofold: the "getting it out" or drafting stage, which often consists of that initial burst of poetic energy, and the crafting or aesthetic stage. The two frequently intertwine to create an experience of hard work and ecstasy. The poet is married to that poem for the entire period of revision and is often obsessed with language, trying to get it "right." She or he thinks about the poem constantly and continually edits it.

During the revision stage, it is important to get feedback, especially from other poets. It is also necessary for the poet to stand back from the poem, to separate from it in order to objectively see what needs to be done. One of the most difficult things for a poet to do sometimes is to forsake a favorite line or stanza for the sake of the poem. However, the poet must be objective enough to recognize when certain words or images are a burden to the poem and not an enhancement. Any wasteful words must be discarded.

Lastly, the poet must take responsibility for his or her words. A poem can and should affect people profoundly. It can cause emotional responses or even move people to action. This is not to be taken lightly. Poetry is also a survival tool, because it can provide an emotional release, solve a problem, or fill a void within oneself. It is a friend to the writer. It exercises the imagination and keeps the spirit alive. It connects people and things in the universe. It is an artistic expression in its purest form.

After discussing the meaning of poetry, students look at short definitions of poetry terms.

POETRY TERMS

Alliteration	— Repetition of consonant sounds
Assonance	— Repetition of vowel sounds
End stop line	— A line that is a complete unit when read aloud
Enjambment	— A line or stanza that doesn't stop, but flows into the next line
Figurative language	— Figures of speech such as the above
Foot	— Unit used to measure meter
Free verse	— Open form with no set meter or rhyme
Imagery	— Pictures made out of words; figurative language used to describe ordinary things
Lyrical poem	— A poem that is musical, meditative, and imagistic
Metaphor	— Comparison without using "like" or "as"
Meter	— Measured pattern of stressed and unstressed syllables
Narrative poem	— A poem that tells a story
Persona	— Writing in someone else's voice using his or her point of view
Personification	— Giving human characteristics to animals or objects
Rhyme	— Repeated sounds
Rhythm	— A set or subtle pattern sometimes using repetition or varied line lengths
Simile	— Comparison using "like" or "as"
Stanza	— A unit of awareness, such as a paragraph in prose
Symbol	— Something representing another larger thing or idea
Tone	— The author's conveyed attitude

To be good poets, students needed to read poetry—good poetry. So as part of their mandatory assignments, ask students to read specific poems from the book *The Language of Life* and critique them. Their packet also includes the following "Poetry Discussion Sheet" that they need to fill out before coming to class.

POEM DISCUSSION SHEET

1. What is this poem about? Is there more than one meaning? How are the meanings layered?

2. What is the poet's tone?
3. What details does the poet use? What colors, descriptions, senses does he or she use?
4. What images does the poet use? Does he or she use figurative language to create those images, and how? What do the images mean?
5. How does the poem elicit an emotional response?
6. Discuss the crafting of the poem. How do the lines and stanzas work? Does the poem tell a story or recreate an experience, and how?
7. Notice the rhythm of the poem. How is it achieved?
8. How is the poem universal? How does it speak to you personally?

Have the students discuss the poems and review their poetry discussion sheets in small groups and then as a whole class. This helps them to go deeper into the meaning and craft of poems and figure these things out on their own first, and then with their peers. They can keep adding to their initial thoughts after hearing from others.

The professor only weighs in after the students present their findings to the class. That way the students don't depend on their professor to be able to understand a poem. They must master the tools to receive and interpret poems on their own, and they get credit for filling out the sheets. The final question is particularly important because it allows students to see how they can enter a poem and relate it to their own lives.

Another assignment is for students to keep a daily journal. Give them unique topics to choose from that stimulate ideas, such as: "Have a conversation with the grass, a tree, or your pet. What can you learn about that world?" Also allow them to make up their own topics and get credit. This is a great way to warm up their writing, like exercising or gestating ideas for a poem.

The last form in the poetry packet, aside from the actual writing exercises, is a critiquing form. It's important to talk about how to critique each other's work in a positive, encouraging way, as well as in a constructive, critical way.

POETRY-WRITING WORKSHOP CRITIQUING SESSION

1. What does the poem say to you?
2. What lines or images work well?
3. What details capture your interest?
4. Is the poem sensual? How?
5. How does the poem convey emotion?
6. Comment on the structure of the poem and the line.
7. Does the rhythm work?
8. What confuses you?

9. What would you like to know more about?
10. Is there any abstract language and are there any clichés?
11. How is the poem meaningful and universal?

Once students have their initial discussion about poetry and go over the forms in the poetry packet, they begin writing poems. Remind them of what the poet Lucille Clifton said: "Let the poem find you," and that Stanley Kunitz also said that poets don't always get to choose what they write about; the poem chooses them.

Each writing assignment begins in class. Everyone writes for about fifteen to twenty minutes. Give the students open-ended prompts, like in the exercises included in this chapter, and allow them to decide on a specific topic or just let a topic come to them. Either way, encourage them to allow the poem to go in whatever direction it wants to go.

Then students finish and revise their poems at home. Have them sign up for a critiquing session and ask them to bring in copies for everyone to follow along during their fifteen- to twenty-minute session. It usually works best to critique poems as a whole class, as opposed to having students do that in groups, as they do with stories, memoirs, and dramatic scenes. That way, the professor can be more fully involved, rather than just circulating and monitoring the process.

Each critiquing session starts with the student reading her or his poem aloud. After hearing the poem in the poet's voice, ask another student of the opposite sex to reread the poem aloud. That way, the student poet, as well as the class, can hear the poem in a voice completely different from his or her own.

During critiquing sessions it is supportive for students to say what they observe in the poem, what they like, as well as what is not working for them as readers. It is not useful to say that nothing is wrong with the poem, since poems aren't "right" or "wrong." It helps for them to just react to the poem as audience members. They can ask themselves, "What is this poem about? Does the poem move me? Why?"

It's also important to remind students to refer to the "I" in the poems as the "speaker" and not to assume that the poem is about the author's life. This goes for the poems they read from books, as well.

It can be helpful to allow the student poet to participate in the discussion, providing that she or he is not defensive. That way, the student poet can answer questions at the moment other students ask them or explain anything that's confusing. It is very important, though, that the student poet listen to what people say, but he or she doesn't have to agree with them or change the poem.

Students learn that many professional poets are in writing groups, and sometimes the feedback varies from person to person. But a serious poet should not dismiss anything someone says. She or he should definitely consider it, but doesn't have to use the feedback.

They also learn that sometimes when a poet changes something based on another poet's suggestion and sits with that change for a while, the poet might realize that the poem is better. With craft, the poem is in charge, and sometimes poets have to change something that they love about a poem because it's just not working. They must honor what the poem needs.

At the end of the critiquing session, the professor checks in with the student poet to see how he or she feels about the feedback and then asks the class to give the copies of the poem back to the student with comments and their signature. That way, the student poet has notes to use for revision, and the class becomes a community of writers. Throughout the critiquing process, students also have the option of getting feedback on their work from the professor during office hours.

By the end of the poetry portion of the course, students need to have written six or eight new drafts but only need to polish three of them. Then they turn in all their work in a pocket portfolio with the polished pieces on the right and the others on the left. Drafts are stapled underneath the final copies.

Even if a professor is fundamentally opposed to grading poetry, in a college class she or he is stuck with it. So one of the best solutions is to grade on both effort and craft. If the student poet shows that she or he has done a good deal of revision, this should be considered. But the crafting of the final pieces is most important. If the student has been paying attention, he or she will not be using clichés and will, instead, be using concrete images, for example.

It is also important to remember that sometimes it takes years for a poet to develop his or her voice. If the final poems are anywhere from decent to great, consider giving the student an A on the portfolio with lots of positive comments and suggestions. If little effort has been made or if the poems lack specific details or are rhyming jingles, consider giving the student a B. However, if the portfolio is missing any of the assignments, the student should not get a passing grade.

The idea of grading the whole portfolio is better than grading the individual poems. That way students won't feel like they're vulnerable in a poem and that the professor isn't sensitive to that vulnerability. No one should have to walk away with hurt feelings; instead, she or he should be excited to revise the poems.

This is just the beginning of a poet's life. Becoming steeped in poetry also means creating products and experiencing poetry out in the world. Some classes might put together anthologies. Some classes might go on field trips to poetry readings, and some students might read their poems at "open mics." It's a good idea to require students to go to at least three poetry readings in the community during the semester.

During the years as a professor at Oxnard College, one class took a field trip to hear Allen Ginsberg read at University of California, Santa Barbara. One class read their own poetry at a local gallery. They invited their friends and had a great little reception. Several classes made anthologies.

The most special events, though, happened at the Carnegie Art Museum in Oxnard. Three years in a row, students from Oxnard College creative writing classes were invited to read a few poems for the Arcade Poetry Series along with two professional poets during National Poetry Month. They received small honoraria and subscriptions to *Poets & Writers Magazine*.

Over the years, it was exciting to see students enroll in the advanced creative writing course, which was basically an independent study where they read, critiqued, and wrote a lot of poems. Some students went on to four-year universities and continued writing and studying poetry. They sent their poems back; they kept coming and coming, and they kept getting better and better. Some students even got their poems published. That's success—students who become committed poets, joining the ranks of muses.

This chapter is dedicated to Steve Kowit—a friend, poet, editor, critic, and dedicated college teacher, who died suddenly in 2015. His love for poetry inspired his colleagues as well as thousands of emerging poets.

SAMPLE WRITING EXERCISES

For each of these exercises, there is only one model poem presented. Professors can use their own published poems for additional models or can find other model poems in Bill Moyers's *Language of Life: A Festival of Poets*. A DVD is also available.

1) Imagination: Poetry of Place—Remembering

The imagination is an essential tool for writing poetry. People use their imaginations constantly to pretend, to make decisions, to daydream, to discover, to create, and to empathize. No one can be an artist if she or he cannot envision what he or she wants to create. One way to use the imagination is by remembering. In this exercise, students will draw on memories to create poetry of place.

First, have a student volunteer read a model poem from *The Language of Life* that is centered around specific places.

"Remember," by Joy Harjo

Remember the sky that you were born under,
know each of the star's stories.

Remember the moon, know who she is. I met her
in a bar once in Iowa City.
Remember the sun's birth at dawn, that is the
strongest point of time. Remember sundown
and the giving away to night.
Remember your birth, how your mother struggled
to give you form and breath. You are evidence of
her life, and her mother's, and hers.
Remember your father. He is your life, also.
Remember the earth whose skin you are:
red earth, black earth, yellow earth, white earth
brown earth, we are earth.
Remember the plants, trees, animal life who all have their
tribes, their families, their histories, too. Talk to them,
listen to them. They are alive poems.
Remember the wind. Remember her voice. She knows the
origin of this universe. I heard her singing Kiowa war
dance songs at the corner of Fourth and Central once.
Remember that you are all people and that all people are you.
Remember that you are this universe and that this universe is you.
Remember that all is in motion, is growing, is you.
Remember that language comes from this.
Remember the dance that language is, that life is.
Remember.

Talk about the rich description of places in this poem. The poet describes the sky, the moon, the earth, the wind—essentially everything that gives life. She only references a few specific places such as "the corner of Fourth and Central . . . ," but that's enough since the entire poem describes things in the universe as the setting.

The assignment is to write a poem that draws on memories of a place. Students can use their imaginations to enhance that place and embellish the memory with details they've forgotten. Tell them to create a full picture with detailed descriptions of both the place and any people who were there with them. Past or present tense is fine.

Here's a poem by a student that uses the imagination to reveal a poem of place.

"Prince William," by Vanessa

I love the busy forest in my uncle's backyard.
The mango orange, pollen yellow, and tomato red leaves
even feel healthier than those I've left back home.
Their felt-backed veins, soft like a new cotton shirt.

The dribbling creek, marred by a dusty bike trail
whispers condolences to the overturned turtle
smelly in its dead, broken shell that rests on its banks,
surrounded by the water-polished rocks
that shine brighter than my glinting bracelet.

The birds yell, alerting me to the coming storm.
I can already taste it; muggy, yet still fresh.
The shudder in my chest resounds
the thunder that starts it all.
I love summer in Virginia.

2) Imagery: Somewhere Outside in the City or in Nature

Establish that imagery is the language of poetry, the stuff that poetry is made out of. Then have a student volunteer to read the first stanza of a long model poem from *The Language of Life* that has rich imagery.

from "The Legend," by Garrett Hongo

In Chicago, it is snowing softly
and a man has just done his wash for the week.
He steps into the twilight of early evening,
carrying a wrinkled shopping bag
full of neatly folded clothes,
and, for a moment, enjoys
the feel of warm laundry and crinkled paper,
flannellike against his gloveless hands.
There's a Rembrandt glow on his face,
a triangle of orange in the hollow of his cheek
as a last flash of sunset
blazes the storefronts and lit windows of the street.

This poem takes place in an urban area on a winter evening. Talk about the specific images, such as "He steps into the twilight of early evening" and "There's a Rembrandt glow on his face/a triangle of orange in the hollow of his cheek." There are also lots of details, such as "carrying a wrinkled shopping bag" and "the feel of warm laundry and crinkled paper."

Then ask the students to write about a time when they were outside in an urban setting like in a park in the middle of a city. Or they can write about going out into nature to the beach or a wooded area or even their backyard.

Ask them to become aware of every detail and every sense and to become one with their surroundings in their poems, creating images to capture the place and mood. They can include any action that is occurring, like waves crashing or wind blowing or snow falling—whatever is there. They need to remember to use their five senses to describe the experience.

Here's a student poem that weaves in and out of natural and urban settings with great images like "I encounter a lofty yellow flower/under the reign of a sprinkler."

"Pity the American Dandelion," by Alina

The dandelions grow longer
here in Los Angeles;
I flee to the market for milk
to make hot chocolate,
dark or with marshmallows,
because the jade house is frigid.

During the premature spring
here in Los Angeles,
I encounter a lofty yellow flower
under the reign of a sprinkler:
a delicious dandelion,
wet and seasoned.

Harvested from its roadside habitat
here in Los Angeles,
the flower accompanies me
to the store, out the checkout line
and with a carton of milk,
we stroll suburban roads.

Florets have matured into "clocks"
here in Los Angeles,
it's time to make a wish and blow:
Certainty in an uncertain world!
Rapt with manifest destiny,
the feathers take flight.

Standing in the sun, on the lawn
here in Los Angeles,
I stare at the herb, I've heard
they are great in salads:
bittersweet and endearing,
alongside radishes.

Although sweltering in smog
here in Los Angeles,
I wonder how my friend fares,
and my curiosity knows
no cure other than to taste
this tainted blossom.

3) Color: An Event Captured in a Colored Photo

A camera can capture a person or a group of people and immortalize them in that moment. When people look at photographs, their memories are instantly revived. They become nostalgic, sometimes sad or happy or angry about certain experiences they have had. Regardless of the situation, the photograph allows them to focus in on a moment in time—in full Kodacolor. Poets create from that moment. They recreate memories, disclose secrets, or create imaginary stories, if they don't have real ones.

Have a student volunteer to read this model poem from *The Language of Life*.

"I Go Back to May 1937," by Sharon Olds

I see them standing at the formal gates of their colleges,
I see my father strolling out
under the ochre sandstone arch, the
red tiles glinting like bent
plates of blood behind his head, I
see my mother with a few light books at her hip
standing at the pillar made of tiny bricks with the
wrought-iron gate still open behind her, its
sword-tips black in the May air,
they are about to graduate, they are about to get married,
they are kids, they are dumb, all they know is they are
innocent, they would never hurt anybody.
I want to go up to them and say Stop,
don't do it—she's the wrong woman,
he's the wrong man, you are going to do things
you cannot imagine you would ever do,
you are going to do bad things to children,
you are going to suffer in ways you never heard of,
you are going to want to die. I want to go
up to them there in the late May sunlight and say it,
her hungry pretty blank face turning to me,
her pitiful beautiful untouched body,
his arrogant handsome blind face turning to me,
his pitiful beautiful untouched body,
but I don't do it. I want to live. I
take them up like the male and female
paper dolls and bang them together
at the hips like chips of flint as if to
strike sparks from them, I say
Do what you are going to do, and I will tell about it.

Here, the poet uses "ochre" to describe an earthy color in the phrase, "under the ochre sandstone arch . . ." and "red" in the phrase "red tiles glinting. . . ."

The entire poem is a photograph of the speaker's parents, describing how they look against a college setting before they are married, and it goes on to predict their future.

For this lesson, tell students to go through their own collection of photographs or through their memory base of events in their lives and capsulize one in a poem. Ask them to focus in on the event, what's happening, who is there, and where they are in relation to the photo. To enrich the poem, they can make it a colored photo. Most of all, they need to make the event significant, like a rite of passage or a celebration.

Here's a poem by a student that talks about the stages of a love relationship. She likens it to "new life/like bloody, unsteady lambs that stink up the farm." As the relationship progresses, it becomes like climbing a mountain, noticing the "blue blue sky above/and the green slopes below." Both lines use color, and "blue" is repeated for emphasis. The poem is wonderfully rendered with rich descriptions.

"Love Like," by Fiona Cox

I want to do to you what spring does
to the cherry trees.
—Pablo Neruda

In the beginning
I want that AprilMayJune kind of love
like new life,
like bloody, unsteady lambs that stink up the farm.
I want that pounding Pacific wave love
that wrenches me from my board and hurtles me, circling
up, up onto the sand.

And then maybe love like a mountain climb,
sometimes agony and always requiring effort and strength
yet always absolutely worth it,
with the blue blue sky above,
the green slopes below
and a quietly shining brook
of your understanding and continuous friendship
all the way to the summit
and down the other side,
leaning in,
hand in familiar hand.

4) Emotions: Expressing Feelings through the Use of Five Senses

First talk about the importance of expressing feelings in poems. This can be done, of course, without stating the feelings, but by telling a story and using the five senses to make the feelings come through the poem. Then ask a student to read a model poem from *The Language of Life*.

"The Gift," by Li-Young Lee

To pull the metal splinter from my palm
my father recited a story in a low voice.
I watched his lovely face and not the blade.
Before the story ended, he'd removed
the iron sliver I thought I'd die from.

I can't remember the tale,
but hear his voice still, a well
of dark water, a prayer.
And I recall his hands,
two measures of tenderness
he laid against my face,
the flames of discipline
he raised above my head.

Had you entered that afternoon
you would have thought you saw a man
planting something in a boy's palm,
a silver tear, a tiny flame.
Had you followed that boy
you would have arrived here,
where I bend over my wife's right hand.

Look how I shave her thumbnail down
so carefully she feels no pain.
Watch as I lift the splinter out.
I was seven when my father
took my hand like this,
and I did not hold that shard
between my fingers and think,
Metal that will bury me,
christen it Little Assassin,
Ore Going Deep for My Heart.
And I did not lift up my wound and cry,
Death visited here!
I did what a child does
when he's given something to keep.
I kissed my father.

This poem tells an endearing story and uses strong imagery throughout, such as describing something being planted in the boy's palm: "a silver tear, a tiny flame." The boy can *feel* "the iron sliver I thought I'd die from," but his father takes it out so gently that his hands are "two measures of tenderness."

When the father tells the boy a story, he can also *hear* his father's voice, "a well/of dark water, a prayer." The narrative poem is so vivid that the reader can *see* what the *boy* sees happening. The love that the boy has for his father comes pouring through the poem, without the poet stating it.

The assignment is to write a poem where strong emotions come through by using the five senses. Tell the students to make the poem lyrical—musical, capturing a meditative moment or moments. It can also have a narrative thread to it.

Here's a poem by a student where the speaker mourns the breakup of a relationship and has to move out as a result. She *sees* the things she has to take with her, *smells* her partner's shampoo, stating "For months, I'm going to smell like you," *hears* the "phone burning my ear" and *feels* the wet towel, the tears, and "the dry mouth, aching chest."

"Moving Day," by Fiona

So it has come to this:
suitcases and divided trinkets.
Today I shall extract myself from you.

In the bathroom.
The razor we shared.
My shampoo, originally your brand.
For months, I am going to smell like you.

My towel is hooked up next to yours.
I drop it, damp, in the laundry basket
because I know you would hate that.

I rifle through jewelry drawers.
Yours. Mine.
Mine? Yours?

The matching silver promise rings.
I leave them, empty, on the shelf.

You said I guess my heart wasn't in it.
I said I guess mine was.
I was clawing for solid walls,
huddled in the crack between bed and wall,
phone burning my ear,
palms pushing tears back into my eyes,
dry mouth, aching chest,
can't swallow, can't allow it in.

5) Figurative Language: Similes and Personification

Discuss the meaning of simile and come up with an example, such as "Her cheeks are as red as pomegranates." Tell the students that similes create vivid and sometimes unusual pictures, instant images. Similes should be fresh and unique and should stretch the imagination. They don't have to make sense on a literal level, and they usually don't. Yet the reader can relate to the image, can imagine it, and can find it fascinating.

Using personification also creates images. An example is "The sun parts the clouds with its fingers." Everyone knows that the sun doesn't have fingers, but the image works, and the reader accepts it. Have a student read a model poem from *The Language of Life*.

"Peonies at Dusk," by Jane Kenyon

White peonies blooming along the porch
send out light
while the rest of the yard grows dim.

Outrageous flowers as big as human
heads! They staggered
by their own luxuriance: I had
to prop them up with stakes and twine.

The moist air intensifies their scent,
and the moon moves around the barn
to find out what it's coming from.

In the darkening June evening
I draw a blossom near, and bending close
search it as a woman searches
a loved one's face.

Discuss the figurative language in this poem. The poet writes, "Outrageous flowers as big as human/heads! . . ." That's clearly a simile. She also uses personification when she writes, "The moist air intensifies their scent/and the moon moves around the barn/to find out what it's coming from." The implication is that the moon is curious to find out about the scent, like a person would be.

The assignment is to write a poem using either similes or personification or both. Again, tell the students to make the poem lyrical—musical, capturing a meditative moment or moments. They can also add a narrative thread to it, if they want.

Here's a poem by a student that personifies a notebook the speaker is using to write in. She writes that the book "will not judge me" and the words "open their mouths wide/screaming the most intimate secrets." In the end, the book speaks to the reader.

"To My Book," by Krista

no volume to this paper
screaming at you keeps getting better
indestructible ear drums
always ready for combat
to perceive my war-like thoughts
like a maniac imprisoned in your pages
I transfer them to you
knowing that you will not judge me
at times I cannot speak out loud
as if my vocal chords went on vacation
to the side of my body
where it tells me to write it down
these words I write
open their mouths wide
screaming the most intimate secrets
I am the only one here
I am the listener
I know beautiful secrets

Chapter Five

I Remember

Cedar Community Center for Senior Citizens

> *a man with a satchel in his hand*
> *with the look of a doctor on his face,*
> *both conscious and detached,*
> *walks the muddy road,*
> *unaware of the mighty apparition ahead of him,*
> *humming gleefully*
>
> —Esther, *from* "God of Our Fathers"

"The Kids' Shelter and the Senior Center," by Shelley Savren

Like a tiger racing to another world,
Heather skips in her rumpled dress and orange bow.

She sleeps in the family station wagon,
writes poems about tigers roaming

and draws pictures of cubs playing in her lap.
Esther rouges her cheeks into ruddy bloom.

Her silver bun forms a hive behind her head.
She talks of sculpting hair in Germany,

quotes Buddha and Gurdjieff.
At home she feeds me strudel, tea

and *shpiels* about my soulmate.
Heather shows up at my college class

a decade later, her hair cropped and tinted orange
on top. Esther turns ninety and dances *Horah*

a month before she dies, kicking up her legs
like a tiger racing to another world.

Cedar Community Center for Senior Citizens in San Diego was an organization where people over sixty years of age came to participate in a variety of activities. They were active seniors from all kinds of backgrounds who were not working at jobs and wanted enrichment in their lives. In the late 1970s, Community Arts sponsored a two-hour poetry-writing workshop there twice a week with the same group of students for one year. This was as an opportunity to draw from their worldly experiences and memories as subject matter for their poems. Here was a group of people that knew about living. They had lots of stories to tell and much to teach.

Thirty-two people showed up at the first workshop. After that, the usual count was around ten or twelve, but a handful stuck it out for the entire year. Most of the students were well educated, but not many had advanced degrees, something that was not uncommon for that generation. But they all could write well. In fact, one of the students, Ruth, was a published playwright. She'd written one-act plays that were published by Baker's Royalty Plays in Boston and were produced in San Diego theaters. The class went to one of the productions.

In the late 1970s, one of the challenges was to teach these students to "unlearn" what they knew about poetry. Many of them had studied the classics, which gave them a great foundation, but they were also stuck in the mindset that all poetry rhymed, which was not the case for most contemporary poetry. They had to learn that rhyming poetry was great, but sing-songy poetry was not. So they were directed to not use rhyme. But they *were* encouraged to retell their experiences.

The goal for these workshops was to have the students bring their memories to life, to dig back into their past and pull out little gems—to remember the forgotten and give those experiences new energy, new meanings, through poetry.

At Cedar Community Center, they did just that. Jane wrote, "Now all my ports are empty/fishing boats put out to sea/sails bellying in the wind." They were also instructed to write about who they are today and how they experience the world from that perspective. Jane also wrote:

> Yet should my love desire me,
> I'll find him in my kitchen
> in the morning,
> and all he says is
> "Hi, Love."

The most important thing is for these students to write using their imaginations and expressing their thoughts and feelings. Students who are over sixty-five have worlds inside of them to draw from, and the more specific they can be, the easier it is for readers to relate to what they're writing. Because they have so many stories to tell, it's a good idea to suggest that they write narrative poems using concrete language as opposed to abstractions.

It's important to talk about how not everyone can remember all the details in his or her life, and as people grow farther away from an experience, the details become more muffled. They may wonder if their memories are accurate, but that doesn't matter. Remind the students that they can embellish, make up stuff, even put people into the picture who weren't there.

In poetry, what's important is to stay true to the essence of the meaning and true to the emotion—not necessarily to the facts. This notion can be freeing for these students, since so much of their lives has been accumulated in events, and it's hard for any person to remember the details of last month, let alone last year, not to mention fifty years ago.

The class can start with a warm-up exercise where everyone contributes a line to a group poem. Ask them to think about some small thing that they remember from their childhood, like the house they lived in, the color of their bedroom walls, the kind of flowers that grew outside, or a pet they had. They can name the town they lived in. It can be any detail, but they need to make it a rich one, such as, "I slept in a green, plaid, wallpapered room with my brother." Everyone contributes a line to the group poem, which can be typed up for the next session.

Writing starts as a process in these workshops, but the products can be amazing. If there's time, students can also critique the poems that they write. They can type them up and distribute them to the other students for feedback. Ask the students to comment on the details, the images, the form, and the overall music of the poem, and to make suggestions for places to rewrite where the language is too vague or sounds too much like prose.

At Cedar Community Center, everyone was supportive of each other's work, and no one felt pressured to revise. Some did, and some didn't. Soon the poems were flowing in, so each workshop began by reading and critiquing poems written during the previous session. The second hour was devoted to introducing a new poetic concept, reading poems by mostly contemporary poets and giving them open-ended prompts. Everyone wrote for about a half hour and then shared drafts.

For the handful of participants who attended regularly, their commitment was unquestionable. At the end of the workshop, several poems were published in an anthology along with poems from other workshops conducted through Community Arts. They also held a poetry reading at Cedar Community Center, and other seniors came to hear the students' poems. The students took great pride in their work. They were a community of writers and a community of friends.

Then there was Esther. It would be a great oversight not to write about Esther. She was eighty years old when she first came to the workshop. Like several others, she didn't drive, but unlike others, she lived far away, so she only came once. There was something intriguing about her. After the first workshop, she shared that she'd been writing poetry for years and was well educated in many subjects, including Judaism and the philosophies of Gurdjieff. She was absorbed in mysticism. That first discussion initiated a friendship.

There were once-a-month visits at her home in San Diego's North County. She shared an acre of land with her two brothers, daughter, and grandson. Each had her or his own cottage. It was like a commune. She had a wonderful garden with statues of Buddha and other ornaments peeking out among the plants.

She made tea and shared her poetry and her life. Sometimes there would be long walks on the beach. Anyone would want to be like her at age eighty—of great mind and spirit, still pouring out poems. Esther was like a wise sage, with plenty of advice to give to anyone willing to open up to her.

Esther remained a good friend for ten years. When she turned ninety, she could still dance the *Horah* (an Israeli circle dance performed at weddings and other joyous occasions). Her cheeks were as rosy as ever. But then she was diagnosed with cancer and died a month later. She wanted no treatment and said she had made peace with her Maker. Right before she died, her cheeks were still as rosy as ever.

After Esther died, her daughter gave all of her poetry books and her red bookshelf to her poetry teacher and friend. In the end, it was poetry that began that friendship, and poetry that created a bond. This chapter is dedicated to Esther.

SAMPLE WRITING EXERCISES

1) Imagination: Using Symbols to Remember

Talk about symbolism, how a small thing can represent something much larger, like how a wedding ring is a piece of jewelry, but it represents commitment and love. An American flag is just a piece of cloth with a nice design, but it is a symbol of freedom or patriotism.

There are symbols throughout everyone's life. Different objects can remind people of different times in their lives, like a quilt on a bed can remind them of when they were small, and their grandmother tucked them in at night under a big colored quilt she made. Have the students share other examples, and then read model poems. It's a good idea to have copies for the students so they can follow along, or they can volunteer to read them aloud.

"The Mercy," by Philip Levine

The ship that took my mother to Ellis Island
eighty-three years ago was named "The Mercy."
She remembers trying to eat a banana
without first peeling it and seeing her first orange
in the hands of a young Scot, a seaman
who gave her a bite and wiped her mouth for her
with a red bandana and taught her the word,
"orange," saying it patiently over and over.
A long autumn voyage, the days darkening
with the black waters calming as night came on,
then nothing as far as her eyes could see and space
without limit rushing off to the corners
of creation. She prayed in Russian and Yiddish
to find her family in New York, prayers
unheard or misunderstood or perhaps ignored
by all the powers that swept the waves of darkness
before she woke, that kept "The Mercy" afloat
while smallpox raged among the passengers
and crew until the dead were buried at sea
with strange prayers in a tongue she could not fathom.
"The Mercy," I read on the yellowing pages of a book
I located in a windowless room of the library
on 42nd Street, sat thirty-one days
offshore in quarantine before the passengers
disembarked. There a story ends. Other ships
arrived, "Tancred" out of Glasgow, "The Neptune"
registered as Danish, "Umberto IV,"
the list goes on for pages, November gives
way to winter, the sea pounds this alien shore.
Italian miners from Piemonte dig
under towns in western Pennsylvania
only to rediscover the same nightmare
they left at home. A nine-year-old girl travels
all night by train with one suitcase and an orange.
She learns that mercy is something you can eat
again and again while the juice spills over
your chin, you can wipe it away with the back
of your hands and you can never get enough.

In this poem, the name of the ship, "The Mercy," is symbolic, and it's also ironic, because there was little mercy for the immigrants who traveled on that ship to the United States. The poet also likens the word "mercy" to an orange, also symbolic: "while the juice spills over/your chin, you can wipe it away with the back/of your hands and you can never get enough." Then read the next poem.

"My Everything," by Perie Longo

Since I no longer have a husband,
everything else has become mine: always
family and friends, my house, now
my beach, moon, hummingbird, every gopher
who dines on every last root, mine—

especially my field—
the one I've lived behind for forty years,
the one that loves me so much, every day
it combs its hair a different way,
changes shirts to match my mood.

A gate separates us. But I have
the key to enter, roam over its strong breast
whenever I choose. Some mornings
my field sends a red-tail hawk flashing
the sky, a pack of coyotes, noses pressed
against the chain-link fence.

You're beautiful," I sing, charmed
with their wildness, empty-handed.
They skip off sideways at my advance,
return for more.

Last night against the dark sky,
I noticed my oak holding hands with my elm.
At the center of its heart, a light pulsed
from nowhere through thinning leaves.

Just as you left me, field spoke
and scooped me up, my everything.

In this poem, the field has become a symbol of the speaker's old life, "The one I've lived behind for forty years." But now it is also represents her new life where the oak is "holding hands with my elm." It is a symbol of everything wonderful in her life, now that her husband is gone. The field has everything beautiful in it—red-tailed hawks, a pack of coyotes. It is alive, and the speaker realizes, so is she. The poem also uses personification, because the field "combs its hair a different way/changes shirts to match my mood."

After reading the poems, talk with the students about looking back on their lives at whom they knew and may still know, how they have changed or not changed. Talk about the dreams they had that were realized or not realized and the dreams they still have. Ask them to remember an occasion, like a holiday, a milestone, or a special event, and to zoom in on that day, look at what they are wearing, who was there, what was being said, and how they felt.

Tell them to use their imaginations to fill in lapses of memory. They should each write a narrative poem like "The Mercy," but they can use lyrical language in it, as in "My Everything." Remind them to focus on the details and the emotion behind the scenes and to put in symbols, allowing an object or concept to represent something much larger than it is.

When it's time to share, it's usually not enough for them to just read the poems to the group. They have stories to tell that are not in the poem. Ask them to go back and write those stories, as well. Encourage them to also revise the draft they just wrote and to bring it back the following week for the group to critique.

Here's a student poem that also looks into the past. In this poem, the workbench is a symbol for a productive life, a life of hard work.

"Waiting Room," by Jo

I wait like a factory worker
Watching the time clock.
My body bent to the curve
Of the workbench—
My mind reaching
Toward quitting time.
My life squandered
Like a paycheck—
Week after week,
Wasted on living—
Rooms to come home to—
The needs of children
Clothes to be worn
To be mended—outgrown—
Food to be prepared for the table.
Parents weary from working
Children weary from waiting.
Quiet, now—
Hands point Heavenward
Eyes look down—
"Father, we thank Thee—"

2) Five Senses: Hearing the Silence

People come alive when they are described not only by what they look like, but also by what they smell like, what their voices sound like. When someone reads a novel, he or she imagines the protagonist as a whole person. Doing that also makes the world in the book come alive. A landscape takes on scents, sounds, and textures.

Then focus on sounds. Talk about animal and human sounds and the sounds of all living things outside. Then talk about the absence of sound, how that also creates a mood. Silence speaks in its own ways. Ask a volunteer to read the first model poem, which describes a wonderful meadow with a low fog just after deer and birds have left.

"Blue Mesa," by Carolyn Forché

A cottonwood surfaces in the reservoir.
It uproots itself with the breath it has held
since the river rose over the woods.
It rolls with life in the slap of waters.

Trout swim between pines, the fly fisher
whips the lake and the lines
dropped from barely moving boats
tie men to the calm spring canyon.

Here the uprooted cottonwood is silent, "with the breath it has held/since the river rose over the woods." Point out the personification with the cottonwood holding its breath as a human would do. There are other sounds in the poem, but none are loud; even the boats are "barely moving. . . ." And the overall tone created by the silence or soft sounds is one of calmness.

Next, read a poem that talks about a different kind of silence, the silence between two people and the distance it creates. It's from Adrienne Rich's *Twenty-One Love Poems*.

"IX," by Adrienne Rich

Your silence today is a pond where drowned things live
I want to see raised dripping and brought into the sun.
It's not my own face I see there, but other faces,
even your face at another age.
Whatever's lost there is needed by both of us—
a watch of old gold, a water-blurred fever chart,
a key. . . . Even the silt and pebbles of the bottom
deserve their glint of recognition. I fear this silence,
this inarticulate life. I'm waiting
for a wind that will gently open this sheeted water
for once, and show me what I can do
for you, who have often made the unnameable
nameable for others, even for me.

Discuss the mood in this poem. The speaker fears the silence of the other person and fears what it might mean. The beginning line shows hopelessness: "Your silence today is a pond where drowned things live," which, by the way, is a metaphor. The speaker wants words to direct her, but there are none. All of the students can relate to being with someone who is silent, who won't let them in, and how difficult that is.

Ask the students to write poems about quiet things, quiet times, about the silences in nature and the silences between people. Tell them to focus on other senses, as well, like describing what a silent world looks like.

Here's a student poem that gives a wonderful description of a place with sounds and then the same place with silence. The speaker is listening to birdcalls and tires over asphalt from a window. She also observes the silence of "Sparrows, like clothespins stuck on a line," "lawns [that] lie sleepily around calm houses" and "a black-shadowed cat [who] stalks a plump unwary bird." These images are rich and real, making it easy for the reader to see and to *hear*.

"Quiet Neighborhood," by Jane

From my second-story window,
sweet-piercing birdcalls,
slick rush of tires over black asphalt,
planes distantly droning.
Sparrows, like clothespins stuck on a line,
cling to my telephone wires,
explored as one
at some untimely message.
Across the way,
lawns lie sleepily around calm houses;
green-pajamaed children drowsing
at the knees of doting grandparents.
Dark green palm fronds glisten,
a pale butterfly
flits about my red-fruited
pomegranate tree.
While below, just off the driveway,
a black-shadowed cat
stalks a plump unwary bird.

3) Images: Getting Old—What I've Lived Through

Sometimes people create image details with their five senses and sometimes through their imaginations. Sometimes they use similes or metaphors to create images, like Jo did in Exercise 1, when she wrote, "I wait like a factory worker/Watching the time clock." She also had a great image in the next line: "My body bent to the curve/Of the workbench—." Tell the students that their job as poets is to give those pictures language, to put them into words. Then read a model poem that creates a positive image of a woman growing older.

"A Woman Alone," by Denise Levertov

When she cannot be sure
which of two lovers it was with whom she felt
this or that moment of pleasure, of something fiery
streaking from head to heels, the way the white
flame of a cascade streaks a mountainside
seen from a car across a valley, the car
changing gear, skirting a precipice,
climbing . . .
When she can sit or walk for hours after a movie
talking earnestly and with bursts of laughter
with friends, without worrying
that it's late, dinner at midnight, her time
spent without counting the change . . .
When half her bed is covered with books
and no one is kept awake by the reading light
and she disconnects the phone, to sleep till noon . . .
Then
self-pity dries up, a joy
untainted by guilt lifts her.
She has fears, but not about loneliness;
fears about how to deal with the aging
of her body—how to deal
with photographs and the mirror. She feels
so much younger and more beautiful
than she looks. At her happiest
—or even in the midst of
some less than joyful hour, sweating
patiently through a heatwave in the city
or hearing the sparrows at daybreak, dully gray,
toneless, the sound of fatigue—
a kind of sober euphoria makes her believe
in her future as an old woman, a wanderer
seamed and brown,
little luxuries of the middle of life all gone,
watching cities and rivers, people and mountains,
without being watched; not grim nor sad,
an old winedrinking woman, who knows
the old roads, grass-grown, and laughs to herself . . .

She knows it can't be:
that's Mrs. Doasyouwouldbedoneby from
                The Water-Babies,
no one can walk the world any more,
a world of fumes and decibels.
But she thinks maybe
she could get to be tough and wise, some way,
anyway. Now at least
she is past the time of mourning,
now she can say without shame or deceit,
O blessed Solitude.

The woman in this poem may be getting old and is alone, but she's so happy to be by herself that "a joy/untainted by guilt lifts her." And there's this image, a "flame of a cascade streaks a mountainside," creating a feeling of excitement, and the image of "an old woman, a wanderer/seamed and brown," presenting a positive image of a woman getting old.

She still has fears, but her attitude is one of "an old winedrinking woman, who knows/the old roads, grass-grown, and laughs to herself . . ." and one who "now can say without shame or deceit/O blessed Solitude." In the end, the feeling is uplifting.

The next model poem does not paint such a positive image of a woman growing old.

"Mirror," by Sylvia Plath

I am silver and exact. I have no preconceptions.
Whatever you see I swallow immediately
Just as it is, unmisted by love or dislike.
I am not cruel, only truthful—
The eye of a little god, four-cornered.
Most of the time I meditate on the opposite wall.
It is pink, with speckles. I have looked at it so long
I think it is a part of my heart. But it flickers.
Faces and darkness separate us over and over.

Now I am a lake. A woman bends over me,
Searching my reaches for what she really is.
Then she turns to those liars, the candles or the moon.
I see her back, and reflect it faithfully.
She rewards me with tears and an agitation of hands.
I am important to her. She comes and goes.
Each morning it is her face that replaces the darkness.
In me she has drowned a young girl, and in me an old woman
Rises toward her day after day, like a terrible fish.

The poet uses personification here as the speaker *becomes* a mirror in the first stanza and meditates on the wall. It's also a persona poem because the speaker's point of view is from a mirror. And when she becomes a lake, she speaks through it, as well. The last two lines have particularly powerful images: "In me she has drowned a young girl, and in me an old woman/Rises toward her day after day, like a terrible fish." Ask the students what they think those lines mean and what the whole poem is saying.

Have the class explicate the poem to discover that the mirror gives the speaker her true reflection. The lake is a natural mirror, and it also gives a true reflection, unmasked by candlelight or moonlight. Ask the students what happens if a woman goes to a lake and looks into it to see her reflection day after day, year after year. The answer is that she gets old. The feeling here, though, unlike in Denise Levertov's joyous ending, is one of despair.

For this writing exercise, students are to express their feelings by creating images from their own lives or the life of someone else they know. Ask them to examine what they've lived through, like a marriage or having kids or being a grandparent. They can focus on the theme of getting older if they want, but that's just a suggestion.

They can also pick a specific time in their life to examine, such as their teenage or childhood years. Instruct them to focus on creating images that describe a situation or an event and encourage them to consciously use figurative language, especially metaphors or similes.

Here's a poem by a student where the speaker addresses the problem of confusion that sometimes comes with aging. The student poet uses an image of a locked ward and compares dementia to that prison, creating symbolism. She also has a wonderful simile comparing freedom to sunshine. The poem is humorous, an attempt to make light of a grave situation. The humor sticks with the reader and makes him or her laugh.

"Limbo," by Ruth

I have heard it said
that prisoners of war
have much in common
with old people
in locked wards.
Senile dementia
is a prison
and old people
with blue-veined fists
fight shut doors
and want to be free
like sunshine.

Sometimes they manage
to escape
and are picked up
at the bus stop
looking lost
and bewildered
in someone else's clothes.

4) Feelings: When Do I Feel Love, Sorrow, or Anger?

Discuss how a journalist reports facts; his or her stories are void of emotions. But poetry is steeped in emotion, and the poet's job is to deliver the information in such a way that the reader will dive in and cry, laugh, or get angry, for example.

Read model poems, starting with a love poem by Pablo Neruda. Neruda was a Chilean poet who, among other things, was the master of love poems. It's not easy to write a love poem without falling into the trap of making it cliché or sappy. The way to succeed is to make the subject of the passion unique, the story or situation unique, and the language *definitely* unique.

"Wind on the Island," by Pablo Neruda, translated by Donald D. Walsh

The wind is a horse:
hear how he runs
through the sea, through the sky.

He wants to take me: listen
how he roves the world
to take me far away.

Hide me in your arms
just for this night,
while the rain breaks
against sea and earth
its innumerable mouth.

Listen how the wind
calls to me galloping
to take me far away.

With your brow on my brow,
with your mouth on my mouth,
our bodies tied
to the love that consumes us,
let the wind pass
and not take me away.

> Let the wind rush
> crowned with foam,
> let it call me and seek me
> galloping in the shadow,
> while I, sunk
> beneath your big eyes,
> just for this night
> shall rest, my love.

The poem starts with a metaphor comparing the wind to a horse. What a great image! The speaker cries that the wind wants to take him away, so the reader must imagine what is calling the speaker away from his love. He wants his lover to hide him in her arms. The poem is also sensual and describes lying next to his lover, "with your brow on my brow/with your mouth on my mouth/our bodies tied."

Note how that image calls the reader to the bedroom where lovemaking is passionate, but Neruda doesn't lure the reader with sexual descriptions. People's imaginations do that. Nor does he *tell* the reader how to feel. In the end, the speaker sinks beneath his lover's eyes. Wow, now that's a love poem!

Then read a model poem where the speaker is admiring her brother in a photo, and she wants to remember him that way.

"In Praise of My Brother, the Painter," by Michelle Bitting

> How every morning he rose, slave
> to the sound, this endless call to make.
> Mad hatter, dervish sawyer, a primitive
> blur of hands at work: fingers feeding
> the dreamiest bolts through needles,
> vision's machinery. In the photo where
> he stands, fists on hips—defiant, electric
> in his Bowery studio, splotched jeans
> and boots, the clouds of white gesso
> a kind of palette couture—so satisfied
> his look: *Je suis arrivé,* ... And
> this is how I want to remember him.
> Not what a note left like that means.
> Not the slow descent, the pills or piles
> of soiled laundry. Not the dog left barking
> in the kitchen, the bowl with enough grain
> to last. No, I want the beauty, even
> his cursive, the swirling tints
> of parting thought, the art itself: *Dear Sister,*
> *if I could survive this long, you will flourish.*

In this poem, the speaker honors her brother as a painter with "splotched jeans/and boots . . ." and is saddened by his decline and subsequent death. But she will fondly remember the note he left: *Dear Sister/if I could survive this long, you will flourish*." That's where the emotions of loss and sorrow come through in the poem.

Then ask the students to remember a time when they felt a deep emotion, such as sorrow or love, an extreme emotion—not just anger, but *rage*, for example. Ask them to think about what happened that made them feel that way and to write about that experience. Tell them not to state the emotion, but to allow the reader to feel it when the poem is read.

Here is a poem by a student where the reader can see how the speaker is rebelling against aging. The emotion is clearly anger.

"Rebellion," by Ruth

"Do not go gentle into that good night"
Dylan Thomas said.
"Rage, rage against the dying of the light"
and I rage endlessly.
Life is too bloody short
And I am furious!
No time to read all the books
to hear all the music
to see all the paintings
I want to see
or write what I need to write.
My spirit is younger than it ever was,
far out in space beckoning
but my old body
cannot keep up with it
And I am not resigned,
I'm mad as *hell*!

Chapter Six

Every Bird Can Sing
St. Madeline Sophie's Training Center

A sun is like a yellow record.
Frog flip jump.

—Bruce

"Leaping onto a Page," by Shelley Savren

I am rain, blue and red.

They swarmed around me,
touching my hair and clothes, all 56 adults,
grunting or trying to pronounce my name.

When the wind stops blowing it lies down.
It feels cold.
Sometimes the wind sleeps in the air.

Two groups took turns on Tuesdays
at St. Madeline Sophie's Training Center
for the Retarded. Jimmy drew fire engines.
Bill composed pages of lower case b's and l's.

I dreamed about a baby horse.
I was brown, running.

Mike recorded TV schedules. Kathy wrote
inside out as if her whole world stood on a mirror.

The moon is as white as an angel's dress
as blue as a duck pond.
Sometimes the moon is there, and half there,
and the whole round moon there.

Marsi transcribed scripture. Nancy drew
her mother's face with a pointy nose and teeth.

The sun is shiny like a dog.
My favorite food is potato chips.
They taste like a bird.

They taught me to break an image open
and see colors poking out. Circles had smells,
frogs could fly. A touch on the shoulder meant
a poem was ready to leap onto a page.

I was ballet dancing
in a pretty pink silk ballet dress, pink tights
and ballerina shoes. I smelled roses
and dreamed I was in Paris France.
I could feel a man close to me.
He held me so I could pose, so I could dance.

On the first day of the yearlong workshop at St. Madeline Sophie's Training Center, the students swarmed around like bees to honey. It was a little scary, having all fifty-six of them touching hair and stroking arms. But by the second visit, it was obvious that if anyone ever needed to feel loved, this was the place to go. They loved a person for just coming there, for just being a person.

At the time, "retarded" was the appropriate term, and its use was not considered disrespectful to this group of people; today, "developmentally disabled" is the term that's used. Either way, this was a unique population to be teaching poetry writing to. But any visiting poet just needed to know about poetry and have the determination to work with this group. There was a lot to learn, and the students at St. Madeline Sophie's were great teachers and a huge inspiration.

The abilities of the students in each of the two-hour weekly classes ranged from not being potty-trained and not being able to hold a pencil or write anything at all to being able to write at about a second- or third-grade level. The range in between was vast. Some of the students just came, sat, and smiled. Some drew stick figure pictures, line drawings, or circles. Others were tracking and were able to copy what was written from their dictation.

Some wrote inside out or upside down, if one can imagine that. Some wrote their name over and over, or just letters. Some were able to write one sentence, one image, one amazing metaphor. And a handful actually wrote short poems. But one way or another, each student communicated from her or his own world.

What was most amazing was their innocence, the childlike qualities they brought to bear. They had the most fascinating imaginations. No stretch was too great. Their similes were effortless. Shirlene wrote, "The sun is shiny like a dog." Robert wrote, "The sun is yellow like the ribbons on shoes, blouses." Cathy wrote:

Sunburn sunburn
the earth the earth
on my nose on my nose
wind sweater wind sweater
knitting knitting.

Their associations leaped like streams of consciousness, almost like transcendental leaps, in some cases. Then there were those students who revealed deep thoughts and feelings that might not have been expressed before. Mary wrote:

I am in bed asleep.
I see red and yellow
and nobody knows
what's happening now
but me. But one thing I do know. One thing
that when I wake up, my self is a lot more
and nobody really cares at all.

The workshops were divided into two groups, chosen arbitrarily, and each group had a one-hour poetry-writing lesson. There was no aide or assistant present. The students sat around one extremely long table and wrote on large sheets of lined paper, like the ones used in primary grades. The sessions were actually structured like those in elementary school.

They started with a group poem, but it was obvious that they were at such different levels that they needed to work independently. No one had taught them poetry before, and they loved hearing the poems read to them. They also loved writing and proved that anyone can learn to write poetry.

With this population, it's a good idea to begin with an open-ended writing prompt and some direction for writing. It's important not to dictate too specific a topic and to allow the students to write whatever they want. Even if you need to give them first lines, they can use their imaginations and create from their own experiences. There are no rules. Don't stress form, but design the lessons to introduce poetics, such as imagery, metaphor, simile, the use of the five senses, and expression of feelings.

Many of the students will enjoy looking outside for stimulation, and some will get going right away and write on their own. Others may sit patiently waiting to give dictation. Write down what they say verbatim, skipping lines, so that they can copy the words if they choose to and make the poem their own. Some of them will just write what appears to be nonsense. Just know that they're communicating, and for whatever it seems to be, it is a poem to them.

Allow about twenty minutes for writing. Then circle around the table again. This time, touch their shoulders one at a time, which means it's their turn to read. Some of the students will read what they wrote, some will choose to remain silent, and some might make up something else on the spot, pretending to read what's on the page. But they will all take pride in their poems.

At the end of every session at St. Madeline's, the poems were collected. It was hard to make copies because they were on large sheets of paper, and the way they wrote words or drew pictures was really too unique to just type up. Instead, they were kept safe in a file cabinet because someday, that experience and those poems might be written in a book. Years have passed, and they are owed their voices here and now.

SAMPLE WRITING EXERCISES

1) Imagination and Poems of Place: Where Does Music Take Us?

Tell the students that if they go to a restaurant, they can imagine what the food will taste like before they order it. If it's raining outside, they can imagine how it feels to be wet. That's real, because they've been wet before, but if they imagine being a frog, that's make-believe, because none of them has been a frog before.

They can also imagine themselves being someone else, like their mother or father or a friend. They can imagine themselves being a dog or a bird or a rock or the ocean. They can even imagine being a city or a cloud or the earth. Or they can imagine going someplace fun, a real place or a make-believe place. Ask them what they'd find there.

Next read model poems. The first one is simple enough for them to understand and has great meaning, too. Tell them that there are mountains, snowy mountains, and there are twenty of them. And there is a blackbird, a very still blackbird. The bird is watching, and the reader knows this, because it's moving its eye.

from "Thirteen Ways of Looking at a Blackbird," by Wallace Stevens

I
Among twenty snowy mountains,
The only moving thing
Was the eye of the blackbird.

The next poem is also out in nature. The speaker becomes the flowers; ask the students to imagine that.

"flowers," by Lucille Clifton

here we are
running with the weeds
colors exaggerated
pistils wild
embarrassing the calm family flowers   oh
here we are
flourishing for the field
and the name of the place
is Love.

Then put on instrumental or classical music, something calming and meditative, for about five minutes and ask them to close their eyes and imagine that they are at a special place. Afterward, ask, "What colors did you see? Were you feeling hot, warm, or cold? What sounds did you hear? Who else was there, and what were you doing? Did you feel happy or sad or anything else?"

Now it's time to write a poem and describe the place they imagined using lots of colors, sounds, and feelings. They can be with someone special or all alone. They can make up all kinds of things and put them into their poems.

Here is a student poem that takes us from inside to outside. It is sensual and filled with colors.

"Untitled," by Susie

I am in a studio dancing
to music of the flower and colors
of spring. Rite of Spring

colors of orange, violet, cinnamon
red, blue, navy blue, black

walking across a canyon very
slow on stage. I smell some

smoke coming from the fireplace
up on a hill with some gentle
breezes blowing in fresh air

off the outside porch.

2) Five Senses: Free Association with Strange Objects

Ask the students, "What would it be like if you couldn't taste ice cream; if you couldn't smell flowers; if you couldn't see a sunset; if you couldn't hear the sound of your friend's voice; if you couldn't hug somebody?" This last question will have an impact on them, since they love to touch and hug.

This lesson is an experiential one. Bring in a bag of things with all kinds of smells, sounds, and textures, such as odd-shaped seashells, coral, bells, cotton balls, rubber balls, sticks, garlic, flowers, and so forth. (The contents are similar to those brought in for the GRF in chapter 3, but the students at St. Madeline's choose only one object, and the focus of the lesson is on the senses.)

Ask the students to close their eyes, reach into the bag to retrieve an object and say the first word that comes to mind. Encourage them not to just name the object they think it is. They get to hold onto their objects until the lesson is over. Then read model poems that elaborate on the five senses. The first poem uses the senses of sight, sound, and touch.

from "Sometimes the Moon Sat in the Well at Night," by Marie Howe

Sometimes the moon sat in the well at night.
And when I stirred it with a stick it broke.
If I kept stirring it swirled like white
water, as if water were light, and the stick
a wand that made the light follow, then slow
into water again, un-wobbling, until
the wind moved it.

The poem is very imaginative. It uses the sense of *sight*, because the reader can *see* the moon; the sense of *sound*, because the reader can *hear* the water swirling; and the sense of *touch*, because the reader can *feel* the stick. Tell the students that the poet might have just had a stick to begin with, but the poem is magical because the stick turns into a wand.

Some of the objects in the bag have sounds, so encourage the students to shake their objects and imagine what those sounds could be or what they remind them of. Then read the next model poem. Not only are there sounds of the river outside, but there's the sound of the speaker's breath and also the smell of incense inside.

"This Shore," by Peter Levitt

Deep into night
a dark river
sounds on
and on, only
one man counting
his breath
to hear it. How
many times

does he walk to the window?
How many times return
to the wooden bench
to stare? He
knows the small Spring
petals have washed past him
in the storm-widened
river, he fills
with the smell
of must, of
mud and rain. But
in his blackened room,
the remnant stick
of incense
burns slowly,
releases
its perfume—
there is only
the sharp point
of its glow.

Now it's time to write. This is a free association exercise. Tell the students that they need to use their imaginations and go on a journey with their object. It might change into something else along the way. For example, a cotton ball might change into a cloud or a white field. Or it might remind them of having an earache and putting cotton with medicine into their ear.

A stick might change into a branch of a tree or the tree itself. Or it might remind them of eating a popsicle on a hot summer day. Suggest that they use one or more of their five senses—ideally, at least three of them—and avoid creating lists, such as, I feel this, I smell that, and the like.

Here's a poem by one of the students. She did a good job free-associating whatever she got from the bag, with different foods. Her ending seems disconnected to the poem, but actually, it's not. She is expressing her feelings, probably related to people giving her food.

"Untitled," by Cora

I feel some candy
and marshmallows
and potatoes. And
bananas and tomatoes.
Everybody is nice to me.

3) Feelings and Personification: What Does the Wind Feel Like When It Blows?

Talk about expressing feelings in poems. Tell the students to use their imaginations to figure out how someone else is feeling and put that into their poems. They can even imagine how things feel. This is called personification. For example, ask, "How does the rain feel when it falls and everyone gets mad at it? How does the sun feel when it has to go to sleep at night? How does the earth feel when everyone walks on it?" The students can imagine the answers to these questions.

Then read model poems. The first one shows how the sun feels being alone and how the stream sounds.

"Dusk in Winter," by W. S. Merwin

The sun sets in the cold without friends
Without reproaches after all it has done for us
It goes down believing in nothing
When it has gone I hear the stream running after it
It has brought its flute it is a long way

In this poem, the sun has no friends. The speaker can "hear the stream running after it" once it sets. Explain how that's personification because a stream can't run. For that matter, a sun can't have friends. Then read the next model poem, which is about the wind.

"The Wind That Blows Through Me," by Alicia Ostriker

I feel the hand of God inside my hand
when I write said the old woman
it blows me away like a hat
I'll swear God's needy hand is inside every atom
waving at us hoping we'll wave back

Sometimes I feel the presence
of the goddess inside me said the dark red tulip
and sometimes I see her
waltzing in the world around me
skirts flying though everything looks still

It doesn't matter whether you call the thing
God or goddess those are only words
said the dog panting after a run through the park
and a sprint after a squirrel
theology is bunk but the springtime wind is real

Although the tulip and the dog can't really speak and express thoughts or feelings, in this poem, they do. That's personification. The old woman, the tulip, and the dog describe their experiences with the wind. Each has a different reaction to it.

Now it's time to write. Ask, "What color is the wind? How tall is it? Where does it go when it stops blowing? How do you think it feels when it blows?" Then talk about other elements and ask, "If you were the snow, what would you do?" You could go anywhere and freeze people or make them happy or have snowball fights. Ask, "What would you do if you were the rain?"

Then ask the students to put their ideas into a poem. Remind them to express feelings—either *their* feelings or the element's feelings. In the following poem, this student says, "the wind feels happy." It also uses similes at the beginning, for example, "The wind is as tall as/the blue sky is." You can tell the students that they'll be learning about similes in the next lesson.

"untitled," by Dorothy

The wind is as pale
white as the fingernail
polish is.
The wind is as tall as
the blue sky is.
The wind feels cool on
my face and there are
other times that it feels
cold on my face.
And when it's all over
with the wind feels happy
and seems to go all the way
back to heaven where
it came from
from the very first start.

4) Imagery and Similes: The Moon or Sun or Sky Is Like . . .

First talk about imagery. The students can all see pictures, but now you want them to create pictures made out of words in their poems. Then talk about comparisons and ask them to compare the moon to something. One example is "The moon is like a blooming night flower."

Go on to the stars and then a bird, a rock, their shoes, their hands. With this group, you don't need to worry too much about ordinary comparisons. Some students will do the usual, comparing the sun to fire, but many won't. Their imaginations are quite wild.

Introduce the word simile and give examples: "My hand is as cold as a popsicle," and "The tree is mighty like a Greek statue." Also, look at what someone is wearing and compare his or her sweater to something else using "like" or "as." Then read a model poem that has one big image of watermelons with green stripes.

"Green–Striped Melons," by Jane Hirshfield

They lie
under stars in a field.
They lie under rain in a field.
Under sun.

Some people
are like this as well—
like a painting
hidden beneath another painting.

An unexpected weight
the sign of their ripeness.

The poet imagines the melons lying in a field under the rain and stars and compares this to people who change and ripen, just like the melons do. She uses the simile, "Some people/are like this as well—/like a painting." Then read a model poem that uses similes and nature imagery.

"The Clear Air of October," by Robert Bly

I can see outside the gold wings without birds
Flying around, and the wells of cold water
Without walls standing eighty feet up in the air,
I can feel the crickets' singing carrying them into the sky.

I know these cold shadows are falling for hundreds of miles,
Crossing lawns in tiny towns, and the doors of Catholic churches;
I know the horse of darkness is riding fast to the east,
Carrying a thin man with no coat.

And I know the sun is sinking down great stairs,
Like an executioner with a great blade walking into a cellar,
And the gold animals, the lions, and the zebras, and the pheasants,
Are waiting at the head of the stairs with robbers' eyes.

Talk about the meaning of this poem. Some of the students can figure out that it's about a sunset if you reread the last stanza. Do that for another reason—so they can hear the simile, comparing the sun to an executioner: "the sun is sinking down great stairs/like an executioner with a great blade walking into a cellar." They can use their childlike imaginations to picture the clouds as golden animals capturing the sun for the night.

Now it's time to write poems that create pictures made out of words. Ask the students to think about something in nature, like the sky or the moon, and think about what it reminds them of. The sunrise can remind them of a flower, for example, or the moonlight can remind them of a slow dance or the tree can remind them of apple pie. They can use similes if they want. Review that definition with examples like "The bird's cry is as loud as a siren."

Here is a poem by a student that has wonderful similes, such as "The sky is covering this whole/earth like a screen in a theatre."

"untitled," by Susie

The sky is clear blue like the
kitchen floor is when you look at a
puzzle. The water is very choppy
like a storm that just hit in winter.

The sky is very dark like night
fall of dusk in early morning.
The water is warm like the
bed of an electric blanket.

The sky is covering this whole
earth like a screen in a theater.

Chapter Seven

The Feminist Poet

Women Take Back Words

> "Strong woman, Strong woman," pulse the arteries
> in my head. If I let go of the words, I will tear
> my gray suit off and wail naked by the casket.
>
> —Kata

"Finding the Women's Center," by Shelley Savren

When factory smoke drags
the wind and girdles my lungs
in an iron brace, I can't climb out
of my body to breathe.

After the breakup,
a friend in Cleveland tells me,
It's the '70s. Go to any city.
Find a women's center.
I haul a trailer west,
join a women's rap group.

Someone hands me a knife,
says, *Dig inside.*
You have to open up the hurt.
I write, threading my story
into a circle we share.

In the summer of 1975, the women's movement was in its prime, and San Diego seemed like a great place to be, especially because the ocean was warm enough for swimming. One of the first things on the agenda was to call the local women's center, Center for Women's Studies and Services (CWSS), join a women's consciousness-raising group (also called a "rap" group in the seventies), and offer to teach a course in poetry writing in their Feminist Free University.

They were enthusiastic about the poetry class; however, another woman, Joyce Nower (to whom this book is dedicated), was already teaching poetry writing, so they suggested a class focusing on the work of women poets.

Joyce was the editor of a women's literary magazine called *The Greater Golden Hill Poetry Express*. Her co-editor was leaving town, so she needed someone to take over the job with her. It was an honor. She also had just conceived a new arts organization called The Feminist Poetry and Graphics Center (FPGC) and asked for help launching it. So Joyce became a poetry pal. And over the years, FPGC sponsored several poetry-writing workshops, writing retreats, and poetry readings.

Eventually, involvement at CWSS included writing for and editing a newspaper called *The Longest Revolution* and organizing arts events for women, including poetry readings. Some of the workshops continued to focus on studying poetry by women poets, but most of them were on writing poetry. For several years, the California Arts Council (CAC) sponsored those poetry-writing programs through its Artists-in-Residence programs.

Diverse women were drawn to the women's movement and to CWSS, which provided counseling; referrals for housing, jobs, and health care; and battered women and rape victim support. CWSS also hosted an annual women's arts festival. As with all the activities sponsored by CWSS, the poetry classes attracted women from all walks of life.

Some of the women who came to the workshops were broken inside and were looking for an outlet for expression. They had been silent and were seeking the courage to speak. Some came because they were excited about learning an art form. Some just wanted to make friends. What they all had in common was the desire to express themselves and to learn the craft of poetry writing.

Since so many women come to these types of workshops seeking support, even in the year 2016 and beyond, it's important to begin with a philosophical discussion about the role of a woman as a poet and as an audience member. That includes talking about how a poet must be a full participant of life, in all that's going on in the world, since everything is food for poetry.

Also discuss how life and art are in a constant state of interaction, and that a poet needs to respond to crisis situations—in this case, crises that relate to women's rights—to have an awareness of changes happening around women and to be ready to change themselves and grow. Students learn that when poetry moves people, a poet's obligation becomes one of maintaining that motion and continuing to feed into the process by writing poems. That is the first half of the circle of art.

Participation as audience members is the other half of the circle of art. Students learn that the creation of and the response to poetry are in a constant dialectic and the synthesis is communication. So as writers, they need to take responsibility for their words, because people react to what they've written.

Also discuss how it is their obligation to support each other's efforts if they are to survive as poets and writers because women had been held down for so long—they had no voice, no access to publication, and therefore, no ability to share their words. This, of course, has changed dramatically since 1968, when women's presses first came on the scene. Even in the mid-1970s, most women could not get their work published by mainstream, male-run presses. Women had to work hard to claim the equal ground in the publishing world that they enjoy today.

After the students discuss the philosophical aspect of writing poems, they can move on to the practical aspects. Talk about how poetry has an organic form. In her essay, "Some Notes on Organic Form," Denise Levertov defines organic poetry as "a method . . . of recognizing what we perceive, . . . based on an intuition of an order, a form beyond all forms." First the poet needs to have an experience or a vision, and then she can bring it to speech.

Also discuss the various elements that go into making a poem. Poets journey through the worlds of imagination and senses and discover that poems have textures and are imagistic. Poets also need to pay great attention to the line. Most importantly, discuss how a poem must be true to an emotion, and even if the facts are altered, the poem must be honest and authentic as it unfolds an experience or reveals a truth.

Talk about how poems are revelations, empowering women with the ability of self-expression. This is the key that unlocks a lot of women's minds. This gives women permission to write, to tell their stories—all kinds of stories—happy ones, sad ones, angry ones. These students are all on the journey and are ready to enter a process, allowing themselves to be inspired and write from some place deep inside.

Students also need to be open to having their work critiqued. Discuss how it's important to give positive feedback to each other and to be open to getting rid of the lines they love if they're not serving their poems. They need to be dedicated to language, since crafting is also empowering. It is the task of the poet to pile on and chisel away words until the poem stands up and speaks for itself.

Over the eight years of teaching poetry writing at CWSS and FPGC, women came and went. The classes were usually for two hours and were about eight weeks long. The dynamic changed from group to group, but there were always women who wanted to empower themselves by writing poetry.

They wrote about subjects that were forbidden or secrets such as rape, incest, and battery. They wrote about marriage, divorce, and childbirth. They wrote about their bodies, abortion (legal and illegal), raising children, and loving other women. They also wrote about their gardens, the death of relatives, haircuts, and clothes—subjects that were not unique to women, but that interested them. Nothing was out of bounds, which in itself was liberating.

Teaching poetry to these women helped everyone to find her "voice," and that was contagious. Those workshops fed the students' *and* the workshop leader's writing, and it created sisterhood bonds. Special bonds were formed with another co-founder of FPGC, Mary Montgomery (now Mary Montgomery Contreras), who gave herself fully to poetry and to serving women, and to Lisa Cobbs, a staff member of CWSS, who taught patience and humility.

Those friendships would give anyone the courage to change and grow. And those friendships with Mary and Lisa have endured. This chapter is dedicated to them.

SAMPLE WRITING EXERCISES

1) Imagination: Who Am I?—Defining Ourselves

Talk about the role poetry plays in women's lives, as outlined in the chapter introduction above. Focus on the source of all poetry, which comes from imagination, dreams, and visions. Historically, women have had difficulty defining themselves. Up until well past the second wave of the women's movement in the 1970s, women were defined by who they were in relation to someone else, such as Fred's wife, Jackie's mother, Susan's daughter, the secretary, the first-grade teacher, Mrs. Joseph Smith.

This last identity is particularly effacing. Students today may recall how their mothers or grandmothers were not introduced by their own names. Then ask a volunteer to read a model poem. The first poem focuses on defining a woman. It's a good idea to have copies of these poems for the students.

> **"The woman in the ordinary," by Marge Piercy**
>
> The woman in the ordinary pudgy downcast girl
> is crouching with eyes and muscles clenched.
> Round and pebble smooth she effaces herself
> under ripples of conversation and debate.
> The woman in the block of ivory soap
> has massive thighs that neigh,
> great breasts that blare and strong arms that trumpet.
> The woman of the golden fleece
> laughs uproariously from the belly
> inside the girl who imitates

a Christmas card virgin with glued hands,
who fishes for herself in other's eyes,
who stoops and creeps to make herself smaller.
In her bottled up is a woman peppery as curry,
a yam of a woman of butter and brass,
compounded of acid and sweet like a pineapple,
like a handgrenade set to explode,
like goldenrod ready to bloom.

Next read a poem from *The Common Woman Poems*.

"VII. Vera, from my childhood," by Judy Grahn

Solemnly swearing, to swear as an oath to you
who have somehow gotten to be a pale old woman;
swearing, as if an oath could be wrapped around
your shoulders
like a new coat;
For your 28 dollars a week and the bastard boss
you never let yourself hate;
and the work, all the work you did at home
where you never got paid;
For your mouth that got thinner and thinner
until it disappeared as if you had choked on it,
watching the hard liquor break your fine husband down
into a dead joke.
For the strange mole, like a third eye
right in the middle of your forehead;
for your religion which insisted that people
are beautiful golden birds and must be preserved;
for your persistent nerve
and plain white talk—
the common woman is as common
as good bread
as common as when you couldnt go on
but did.
For all the world we didnt know we held in common
all along
the common woman is as common as the best of bread
and will rise
and will become strong—I swear it to you
I swear it to you on my own head
I swear it to you on my common
woman's
head

Talk about how both of these poems present images of helpless women, but both end with those women taking back their power. Piercy writes, "like a handgrenade set to explode/like goldenrod ready to bloom," and Grahn writes, "the common woman is as common as the best of bread/and will rise/and will become strong—I swear it to you."

Now it's time to write poems where the students give themselves names and identities. These identities can be whoever they are or whoever they want to be. They can define themselves in roles, relationships, or just as themselves. They can also write about the oppressive roles they were put into when they were young and how they are breaking out of them or how they imagine themselves breaking free.

Since these students are a community of writers, everyone writes, including the workshop leader, for about thirty minutes. Then they share their drafts, commenting on what they see working in the poems. Ask them to revise the poems and bring copies for everyone to see the following week.

Also give them an additional assignment—to spend one day over the next week concentrating on one of their five senses, viewing everything in their world through their senses and jotting down what they notice. The idea is to become steeped in the senses. This will get them ready for the next assignment.

Here's a student poem where the speaker starts out helpless in life but, by watching a powerful role model, finds her own strength.

"Untitled," by Kata

The white lace and pink ruffled words stuck in my throat
"Little girls don't climb trees,"
but even then the fragrance of the wood teased my nose.

Years—when the sun through the leaves and branches
formed images of breasts, thighs, faces of goddesses
whose names were forbidden me—I stripped the bark
from twigs as men stripped me of myself, not understanding
my comfort in the luxurious smoothness of the wood.

Yesterday an old woman swept her skirt into a side knot,
ascending the branch above me with one fluid motion,
laughing as she waited for me to follow.

2) Perception: Tributes and Symbols

Begin by critiquing poems that students wrote the prior week. Then move on to the next lesson that focuses on the five senses. Talk about what they observed during the week, and ask them to read what they jotted down.

Everyone is amazed at what they hadn't noticed before, and they all see the value of being open sensually.

This is food for poetry. Ask them to take what they learned and apply it to their bodies. For example, ask, "What does your hair smell like, feel like, and yes, taste like? If you were to describe your hands only by using the sense of smell, how would you do it? How would you describe the feel of your nose?" The idea is to get them to stretch their imaginations.

Then talk about symbols and how they represent something deeper or larger than what's at the surface. A key might represent or be associated with the door to knowledge, for example. They can write a poem celebrating that key, honoring it, or making a tribute to that key. There are also poems that are tributes to a part of the body, symbolizing a tribute to who the speaker really is. Ask a volunteer to read a model poem that is gutsy and is a tribute to the speaker's hips.

"homage to my hips," by Lucille Clifton

these hips are big hips
they need space to
move around in.
they don't fit into little
petty places. these hips
are free hips.
they don't like to be held back.
these hips have never been enslaved,
they go where they want to go
they do what they want to do.
these hips are mighty hips.
these hips are magic hips.
i have known them
to put a spell on a man and
spin him like a top!

On the surface, the hips in this poem are a physical part of the body that help the speaker move, deliver babies, and make love. But in this poem, the hips are also a symbol of freedom for a woman to go where she wants to go and to do what she wants to do without restrictions placed on her by men. Read the next poem, which is about mothering and is an erotic poem at the same time.

"The Breast," by Anne Sexton

This is the key to it.
This is the key to everything.
Preciously.

I am worse than the gamekeeper's children,
picking for dust and bread.
Here I am drumming up perfume.

Let me go down on your carpet,
your straw mattress—whatever's at hand
because the child in me is dying, dying.

It is not that I am cattle to be eaten.
It is not that I am some sort of street.
But your hands found me like an architect.

Jugful of milk! It was yours years ago
when I lived in the valley of my bones,
bones dumb in the swamp. Little playthings.

A xylophone maybe with skin
stretched over it awkwardly.
Only later did it become something real.

Later I measured my size against movie stars.
I didn't measure up. Something between
my shoulders was there. But never enough.

Sure, there was a meadow,
but no young men singing the truth.
Nothing to tell truth by.

Ignorant of men I lay next to my sisters
and rising out of the ashes I cried
my sex will be transfixed!

Now I am your mother, your daughter,
your brand new thing—a snail, a nest.
I am alive when your fingers are.

I wear silk—the cover to uncover—
because silk is what I want you to think of.
But I dislike the cloth. It is too stern.

So tell me anything but track me like a climber
for here is the eye, here is the jewel,
here is the excitement the nipple learns.

I am unbalanced—but I am not mad with snow.
I am mad the way young girls are mad,
with an offering, an offering . . .
I burn the way money burns.

This poem is daring, sensual, and symbolic. The phrase "Jugful of milk! . . ." uses the sense of taste and symbolizes motherhood. The poem is also about identity, since men frequently rate women by their breast size. Sexton writes, "Later I measured my size against movie stars/I didn't measure up. . . ." These lines use the sense of sight. The line, "I am alive when your fingers are" is erotic and uses the sense of touch.

Now it's time to write a poem that's a tribute, honoring a part of their bodies. Ask the students to use one or more of their five senses to describe it. They can also have that body part be a symbol of who they are.

Here's student poem about her hair.

"Haircut," by Kata

I run my hand through my hair
nothing to hang on to
I shake my head without movement
I should never have permitted her to cut it so short
but I let her.

Close to my head
exposing three quarters of each ear
thin feathers of dark blond, beginning
at left side part, waving
back and down, pointing
to the stem of my brain

I allowed her to uncover me
this is what I asked for
I look in the mirror
nothing to hang on to
wondering whether to buy a cheap bandanna

3) Feelings: Taking Back Our Power

Critique the poems from the prior week, then talk about the importance of expressing feelings in poetry. A lot of the poetry written by women in the 1970s was angry poetry. It was radical feminist poetry, personal and political poetry. Women felt disenfranchised from the world of men and wanted to take back their power.

They began by speaking out, demanding their rights and equality with men in all areas, including the family and the workplace. So some of the poetry expressed a condition that women have endured and that they want changed. Ask a volunteer to read the first model poem.

"The Stranger," by Adrienne Rich

Looking as I've looked before, straight down the heart
of the street to the river

walking the rivers of the avenues
feeling the shudder of the caves beneath the asphalt
watching the lights turn on in the towers
walking as I've walked before
like a man, like a woman, in the city
my visionary anger cleansing my sight
and the detailed perceptions of mercy
flowering from that anger

if I come into a room out of the sharp misty light
and hear them talking a dead language
if they ask me my identity
what can I say but
I am the androgyne
I am the living mind you fail to describe
in your dead language
the lost noun, the verb surviving
only in the infinitive
the letters of my name are written under the lids
of the newborn child

Here, the speaker is angry at the world that has defined her and wants to redefine herself with great potential, like that of a newborn child. She sees herself as androgynous, with characteristics of both male and female, as someone new. There is no language to define her. She is becoming someone new.

Then read the next model poem, a more contemporary poem, where the speaker reclaims her power not by demanding justice from men, but by claiming her freedom and reaffirming her own happiness independent of anyone else.

"and in that moment I was happy," by Michelle Bitting

What year it was I can't remember
when the clocks froze I lost track
then woke to find myself prone
full-bodied, tan, on an ideal beach,
sea-shells like smooth white berries ticking away
the collapsed island hours. Even the faces
of beloveds sewn up for now
inside heavy orbs, fruit that sways, oiled
and persistent from tropical branches
until villagers shake them down
and dam the creeks so the children can swim.
I am going nowhere and I like it.
I, a spindle around which salted blue

marimbas, reconstructing heaven,
branding me with vision, the right to overthrow
the cave, the casket past, the possibility of crows.

It's time to write poems that are empowering in some way. They don't have to be angry; they should be passionate, though. They can tell a story, real or imagined, or they can simply say what they want, but the emotion should pour through the poem without stating it.

Here is a poem by a student, where she carefully describes a room the speaker shared with her partner the day after a sleepless night. The last three lines describe the speaker rescuing a helpless girl, perhaps herself reclaiming her own power.

"Remainders," by Betty

The room poses
as for a photograph.
Only the pillows are ajar
where we threw them
their native colors bright
on the white of the bed.
The rocker is emptied
of the clothes we dropped;
the blinds, still, opened,
slash the burning crescent of the sun
a held moment
'til it falls below the hill.
Our mingled breath hangs in the darkened air,
the night you spent sleepless,
reaching once across the world of the bed
to touch my thigh,
and I dreamed
of pulling a waif girl
out of the fire.

4) Imagery, Similes, and Metaphors: Celebration Poems

After critiquing poems from the prior week, talk about images. They can be visual, auditory, tactile, olfactory, or gustatory. One way to create images is using similes or metaphors that might not make sense as linear language. For example, you might say, "The kiss was like a wicked fire" or "The kiss *was* a wicked fire." What comes to mind is passion, a forbidden kiss or maybe a stolen kiss. The students all pitch in and create similes and metaphors. Then have a volunteer read a model poem.

"Black Mother Woman," by Audre Lorde

I cannot recall you gentle
yet through your heavy love
I have become
an image of your once delicate flesh
split with deceitful longings.

When strangers come and compliment me
your aged spirit takes a bow
jingling with pride
but once you hid that secret
in the center of furies
hanging me
with deep breasts and wiry hair
with your own split flesh
and long suffering eyes
buried in myths of little worth.

But I have peeled away your anger
down to its core of love
and look mother
I Am
a dark temple where your true spirit rises
beautiful
and tough as a chestnut
stanchion against your nightmares of weakness
and if my eyes conceal
a squadron of conflicting rebellions
I learned from you
to define myself
through your denials.

This poem is a portrait of the speaker's mother, who may be elderly now or no longer alive. The speaker sees her mother's gentleness and the anger in herself; however, she is peeling away the anger and is not denying herself what her mother denied for *her*self in the past. Talk about the strong imagery: "once delicate flesh/split with deceitful longings," and the powerful metaphor, "I Am/a dark temple where your true spirit rises." This last example is an empowering self-image. It's a celebration. Then read the next model poem.

"The Rapture," by Mary Oliver

All summer
  I wandered the fields
    that were thickening
      every morning,

every rainfall,
  with weeds and blossoms,
    with the long loops
      of the shimmering, and the extravagant—

pale as flames they rose
  and fell back,
    replete and beautiful—
      that was all there was—

and I too
  once or twice, at least,
    felt myself rising,
      my boots

touching suddenly the tops of the weeds,
  the blue and silky air—
    listen,
      passion did it,

called me forth,
  addled me,
    stripped me clean
      then covered me with the cloth of happiness—

I think
  there is no other prize,
    only rapture the gleaming,
      rapture the illogical the weightless—

whether it be for the perfect shapeliness
  of something you love—
    like an old German song—
      or of someone—

or the dark floss of the earth itself,
  heavy and electric.
    At the edge of sweet sanity open
      such wild, blind wings.

In this poem, the speaker immerses herself in images of nature, "the fields/ that were thickening/every morning," and then compares herself to all that beauty, describing how passion "stripped me clean/then covered me with the cloth of happiness—." She states that "there is no other prize/only the rapture the gleaming." At that moment, she is celebrating herself.

Ask the students to write poems that celebrate themselves, to use imagery in their poems and metaphors or similes, if they can. Here's a poem by a student with wonderful images and similes, such as "The reflection is like a mirror," "Diving into the cool water is like jumping/into a glass of iced tea," and "My movements are like fish in the deep sea." A great feeling comes through, and the poem is a celebration.

"Summer," by Dee

Dancing, the trees swing and rustle
The slight breeze is calling.
Green leaves sound are the trees talking.
Summer is here.

The reflection is like a mirror.
You can reach inside and continue moving
Diving into the cool water is like jumping
       into a glass of iced tea.
Refreshing.
The splashes are like waterfalls springing
       up from the surface.

My movements are like fish in the deep sea
contouring my body around the coral.
Reflections of myself swimming, dancing
Warm summer.

Chapter Eight

Freedom Journey
R. J. Donovan Maximum-Security Men's Prison

Within my writing, I am able to break down my prison walls and escape, leave the gangster façade behind.

—Harvey, inmate

"Chino," by Shelley Savren

Water drips from the roof,
a steady plunk on his pillow
and as he turns it hits his face.
Chino reaches for his jeans, buttons
a denim shirt, pulls a beanie
over slicked-back hair.
He flips a switch on the cell wall
and the door unlocks.

He's a petty crime lifer, wears it
on his sleeves, the usual snakes
and sexy female faces. But he can write.
He finds words on the yard
with lizards, roaches, workout weights
and in shadows where the tower guard
can't find him, beneath his beat
of breath, a steady drip of sweat.

He writes about tortillas
his *abuela* made, how she ground
corn with a stone, the color of her eyes
against morning, sun streaks
on her forehead, and crops

he harvested as a kid,
the sweetness of raw kernels,
a breeze that brushed the field
at the end of a hot day,
the ocean he saw only once.

And he writes about a poet,
whose black curls frame her face,
the curve of her neck, his weathered arm
wrapped around her waist.
He is walking. On the streets with her.
Making it. Spilling words
from his broken, innocent mouth.

What it would be like to teach poetry to men who had committed felonies? That world was foreign and scary, too, but the idea of teaching imprisoned men to write poetry was intriguing. There was an opportunity to bring out the side of them that wasn't dark, to help them find a way to express their feelings in poems.

In 1989, ARTSREACH had an Artists-in-Corrections Program, which funded two three-hour workshops once a week, consecutively, over a six-month period at R. J. Donovan Correctional Facility, a maximum-security men's prison in San Diego, about two miles inland from the Mexican border. The two workshops were in different facilities; the first one was held in the evening, and the second was during the day. These were the first workshops to take place at this new prison.

The inmates referred to the prison as "Rock Mountain." It was deliberately located far from any main road, and the last part of the drive to get there was on a deserted, asphalt road complete with tumbleweeds. A mile or two before the entrance, a sign read, "State Prison Property. No Trespassing," in both English and Spanish. The watchtower loomed in the distance, and gray cinderblock walls reached up toward the sky.

Inside the facility, guards carefully checked the red backpack filled with books and issued a name tag and a whistle. To get to the facility or "the yard," where the workshops took place, it was necessary to walk down several metal hallways rimmed with barbed wire.

On the gravel yard, several inmates smoked, worked out with weights and clustered in gangs, according to race: Mexican Mafia, Crips, Bloods, and others. Blacks stayed away from whites and Mexicans and vice versa, and everyone had that over-the-shoulder, watch-your-back stare. The watchtower was on a constant state of alert.

The workshops were held in the craft room, and the artist facilitator taped off areas at the back, marking them "out of bounds" for inmates. The small rooms in each facility had just a table and chairs and a toilet in the corner. Guards patrolled outside.

Inmates wore blue jeans and blue denim shirts. The walls were gray. Everything was gray, so anyone coming in from the outside provided a colorful contrast. But just being a woman in a man's world with only a few female guards was a contrast in itself.

When entering the yard with the artist facilitator, there were frequent catcalls, but inside the workshop room, everything felt safe, and the students showed respect for both the visiting poet and the artist facilitator. Several inmates came initially to check out the woman who was there. Most of them didn't care about poetry or writing at first. They were there for something to do, or rather, something to do with a woman.

When the craft room door shut, all eyes were on each other—the inmates' way of making sure that everyone knew not to mess with them—then their eyes were on the female visiting poet. They all tried to look tough with their tattoos. But never mind the atmosphere. The business there was poetry.

When working in a prison setting, it's essential to get the students to take the workshops seriously. In order to gain their trust, it's important not to know what crimes each inmate has committed. Those crimes usually include burglary, counterfeiting, kidnapping, car theft, rape, and murder—all the really bad stuff. But it's paramount to see the inmates as people, as students of poetry, and to relate to them that way.

Begin by talking about poetry and what it means to them, the usual introduction. Have them keep journals about anything they want, but suggest that they record their thoughts, feelings, and observations. Then begin subsequent workshops with their sharing what they wrote. Also suggest that they not censor their writing. But they need to take responsibility for their words because words create reactions and have consequences.

On the first day, after that initial discussion, tell the students that they are going to take a freedom journey, and they're going to "break out of prison." The goal is really to have them break the prison walls inside themselves by writing poetry. Surprisingly, from the very start, most everyone will write. It won't take long for them to let down their guard with poetry.

Many of the students will want to read what they wrote, so the class needs to discuss ground rules for giving feedback. First they should acknowledge the poem, showing respect and integrity. Then they can ask questions. It's especially important with this population that they give encouraging feedback on drafts so that no one gets defensive. The goal is to get the students to feel good about what they write and safe sharing it with the class. Later on, they can be introduced to critiquing techniques, and they can proceed to critique each other's work.

At "Rock Mountain," each three-hour session went by quickly, and before everyone knew it, the workshops were over. What happened was that the writers, real talented writers, learned an art form of expression. They learned craft and were exposed to great poets. And they all had stories to tell.

They wrote about being on the run, about beatings as a kid, stashing drugs, cops and cuffs and guns. Mike wrote, "I lay across the street in the gutter wishing for death" and "I feel nothing as I slowly raise the cold blue-black steel" and "Bricks and broken windows are a blur." Chino wrote, "The night echoes the silence which is my only refuge/From a past entwined in chaos" and "Dusk, quiet and a light breeze/coming off the face of a large hill."

Nonwriters, illiterate inmates who came, either pretended to write, wrote nonsense, or just absorbed what they could. They came because they loved being in the atmosphere that was created. It was no longer just to check out a woman. It became a sacred time to write and share poetry.

After the workshops ended, some of the students wrote letters to the visiting poet saying how poetry changed them, gave them some sort of purpose for living. Some vowed to continue writing.

The most meaningful letter came from Chino, who stated, "For the past two decades prison gangs have dominated inside these walls, and Shelley had a class of some of the worst members, although she didn't know it, and I don't think it would have mattered to her. What she did was something not short of a miracle. In a few short weeks, her warmth spread and sworn enemies began to share their poems and lives, thus creating not only a comradeship in the class, but within the prison."

Chino had spent his adult life in and out of prison. But the poems he wrote during the workshop showed that he was a gifted poet. Hopefully, he has continued to write. This chapter is dedicated to him.

SAMPLE WRITING EXERCISES

1) Imagination: *Freedom Journey*—A Guided Fantasy

Begin with the use of the imagination, where students give themselves permission to create. This is when you tell them that they're going on a freedom journey and are going to "break out of prison." First read model poems that have direct connections to the students' lives, taking them on journeys.

"Midsummer," by Sam Hamill

Two yearling deer
stood in the heavy falling mist
in the middle of

the road leading in-
to town, brown coats glistening,
huge eyes open wide,

caught in the headlights,
in the first yellowish smear
of coming daybreak.

Twenty feet away,
I finally stopped the car
and sat still inside,

eyes locked together
in a curious searching
with those of the doe.

Minute by minute,
we were transfixed, motionless,
each imagining

the other. And then
the sun peeled back the dark clouds
like a second skin,

and, in unison,
the deer stepped slowly forward,
gently, cautiously,

off the road, into
underbrush that flourishes
along the woods' edge

and vanished in mist.
Dazed, I returned to my day,
to work at hand.

And now, the hour late
in the morning, mist falling
again, I can still

feel my skin prickle
under those beautiful brown
doe-eyes searching me

like a lover's hand,
cautious, slowly exploring
something deep in me

I cannot touch or name.

Talk about the visions in this poem, the landscape with "heavy falling mist." This is the place where the speaker has traveled to in the past. Then he sees a doe, stops his car, and locks eyes with her. It's as if they are communicating with one another. This connection is magical for the speaker, who later in the day can "feel my skin prickle/under those beautiful brown/ doe-eyes searching me."

The next model poem is by Jimmy Santiago Baca, who spent five years in prison on drug charges. While incarcerated, he taught himself to read and began writing poetry. His first book of poetry, *Immigrants in Our Own Land*, published by New Directions, was based on his imprisonment, as much of his other work is. This poem is a keepsake for someone. Ask a volunteer to read it.

"I Am Offering This Poem," by Jimmy Santiago Baca

I am offering this poem to you,
since I have nothing else to give.
Keep it like a warm coat
when winter comes to cover you,
or like a pair of thick socks
the cold cannot bite through,

        I love you,

I have nothing else to give you,
so it is a pot full of yellow corn
to warm your belly in winter,
it is a scarf for your head, to wear
over your hair, to tie up around your face,

        I love you,

Keep it, treasure this as you would
if you were lost, needing direction,
in the wilderness life becomes when mature;
and in the corner of your drawer,
tucked away like a cabin or hogan
in dense trees, come knocking,
and I will answer, give you directions,
and let you warm yourself by this fire,
rest by this fire, and make you feel safe,

        I love you,

It's all I have to give,
and all anyone needs to live,
and to go on living inside,
when the world outside
no longer cares if you live or die;
remember,

        I love you.

In order to free inmates from their prison, have them use their imaginations and travel on a guided fantasy. (This is similar to the guided fantasy used in chapter 3 at Colston School, but it's more appropriate for adults.) Ask the students to close their eyes and imagine the places where you are taking them. Understand that some of them won't do that, and it isn't that they don't trust you. They are simply watching their backs.

The goal is to get them out of their gray world and into a colorful one, a world full of images, sounds, smells, and people they love. First they have to deal with everything they hate in their world and dump it out. Then they have to create something wonderful, something they can keep, a place they can return to. Move slowly on this journey.

Here's how it goes:

Relax, breathe deeply, close your eyes if you feel comfortable doing that. Go into yourself—deeper, deeper inside of yourself. See your colors; hear your music.

Now see yourself in this place. There are things that you hate here, people and stuff that you want to get rid of. Now begin to empty everything out of this place that you want gone. Dump it all into this room. Dump it all into this room.

Now push out these walls. All of the junk is gone. Transform this room into anything you want it to be—another room, an open field—any place you want. Imagine the sounds you hear, the smells, the textures. Notice the details around you, the landscape, the colors.

Now bring in something beautiful.
Now bring in something practical.
Now bring in something relaxing.
Now bring in something challenging.
Now bring in something helpful to someone else.
Now bring in something helpful to yourself.
Now bring in someone you love.

Make something special with that person. Make it together. Each of you put something special into it. Work hard on it; sweat over it; make it perfect; be proud of it.

Now hold what you've made in your hand and look at it. Put it in your mind and register it there. Put it in your heart and store it there. It will always be with you.

Now open your eyes and write.

Tell them to write about their journey. It can be what they dumped out of their lives, a description of the place where they went in their imaginations far away from prison, or about the special thing they made or the person who made it with them. In essence, they can write about any part of the journey and elaborate on it, adding more details.

Give them about a half hour to write. Write with them, so that you become part of this community of writers. After they share and respond to each other's poems, if there's time left, read more poems to them; however, this lesson usually fills up about one and one-half hours, which is half of the workshop time. In some facilities, they can't take a break, because once they walk out the door, they can't return. So just go on to another lesson.

Here's a poem by a student from his guided fantasy:

"Untitled," by Mike

Deep controlled breaths
all is serene and warm
I wonder why I never felt
like this in her presence before
I feel strong and virile
as I gaze into her face
Life is worth living
But where have I been
There is compassion for all mankind
Even the spider web is beautiful
Long graceful fingers clutch my arm
as if she is frightened
Even though the day is bright
I wonder if this is the right time of year
for planting we'll see
Let's go home she says *there is something*
I want to show you
Oh life is grand I can do no wrong
Slowly very slowly with the finality
of the Grim Reaper's blade
the sun peeks over the horizon to wake me.

2) Imagery, Metaphor, and Simile: Writing from Scenic Pictures

Talk about imagery, pictures made out of words, and tell the students that they're going to get inside a scenic picture and imagine their lives there. Then introduce similes, giving the example, "Her cheeks are as soft as cotton," and metaphor, giving the example, "Her cheeks *are* soft cotton." Explain that with metaphors the comparison does not use "like" or "as," and her cheeks *become* soft cotton.

Tell them that creating metaphors and similes sets up a language that automatically produces images, but not all images are metaphors or similes. Then ask a volunteer to read a model poem that creates wonderful scenic images. It also reveals an intimate relationship between the speaker and two Indian ponies.

"A Blessing," by James Wright

Just off the highway to Rochester, Minnesota,
Twilight bounds softly forth on the grass.

And the eyes of those two Indian ponies
Darken with kindness.
They have come gladly out of the willows
To welcome my friend and me.
We step over the barbed wire into the pasture
Where they have been grazing all day, alone.
They ripple tensely, they can hardly contain their happiness
That we have come.
They bow shyly as wet swans. They love each other.
There is no loneliness like theirs.
At home once more,
They begin munching the young tufts of spring in the darkness.
I would like to hold the slenderer one in my arms,
For she has walked over to me
And nuzzled my left hand.
She is black and white,
Her mane falls wild on her forehead,
And the light breeze moves me to caress her long ear
That is delicate as the skin over a girl's wrist.
Suddenly I realize
That if I stepped out of my body I would break
Into blossom.

This poem has two amazing similes, "They bow shyly as wet swans . . ." and "delicate as the skin over a girl's wrist." And the lines "And the eyes of those two Indian ponies/Darken with kindness" create an amazing image.

Then read the next model poem, which describes a scene where the speaker reflects on her past while sitting in a quiet place with "little movement/except for small flickering waves upon the lake." She uses colors: "At all the blue and green and brown the summer/afternoon has to offer . . . ," and names a specific tree: "Lodgepole pines."

"At the Gateway to Desolation Wilderness," by Patrice Vecchione

It is afternoon now, the sun having assumed
its place at the height of the sky, a baked stillness
about this July day. Little movement
except for small flickering waves upon the lake
and the nearly imperceptible glide of wind
through tree branches. Little sound
other than one bird's repeated few syllable call.

For nearly a year, within all the rush and business
of my days, the ones that incessantly hollered,
Hurry, I have waited for a day like this, when everything
appears to linger, the world turning in slow motion
as though nothing bad would ever happen again,

and everything would wait, without impatience,
for everything else, as though this were all there was,
this one any day, this time.

At all the blue and green and brown the summer
afternoon has to offer I look out: swath of lake water
set canyon-deep between two mountain
sides, the stately Lodgepole pines,
the one peak rising to tree-line, its stone
a jutting edge against the bright sky.

Between now and nightfall a bulk of hours
spreads out before me, those recently behind
cluster like shiny beads. It is so still
my mother could be alive.
In the rocker I sit, barely pulsing it back and forth
and a tiny breeze, small as a sleeping child's
breath, comes in through the Dutch door.

There is nowhere I have to go, nearly nowhere
I have ever been, other than here, beside the lake.

Far off a woman's rippling laughter,
once, twice, and then not even the wind's sound.

Point out the simile, "a tiny breeze, small as a sleeping child's/breath. . . ." The images describe a scene that is so quiet there is "little sound/other than one bird's repeated few syllable call."

Then spread out scenic pictures torn from a travel magazine or something similar and ask each student to choose one that speaks to him. The assignment is to get inside the picture, to be there either as an observer, as in "At the Gateway to Desolation Wilderness," or as a participant, as in "A Blessing." Ask, "What does it feel like to be there? What's happening at that moment? What do you see, feel, smell, hear, taste?"

Tell the students that they're going to use imagery to describe the scene and the experience and in order to produce vivid pictures and impressions in the readers' minds. Encourage them to use metaphors and similes if they want. They can imagine themselves or anyone else in that picture.

Here's a student poem with strong images:

"You're Still Alone," by Harvey

Dusk, quiet and a light breeze
coming off the face
of a large hill.
I see the river
through mist-covered trees

as it flows to the south
never ending, never returning.

Sage brush, yucca in early bloom
and boulders in obscure shapes
loom overhead.
Tracks of the bear
overwhelm me with feelings
and a bond—
no, not a bond,
but an awareness of life and death.

A pepper tree,
its fragrance and beauty
are so alluring.
It stops and holds my brother
but only for the moment.
Walking on we sense
rather see the calm
that surrounds the Indian graveyard.

We have come to pay our respects
to Grandfather,
tall, darkened by the sun
and always the impatient green eyes.
The feelings are so intense
that I draw back
as I see the small mound of dirt
that holds the remains
and the reason for my name.

As I leave
I know Grandfather is safe.
Grandfather is
as he always was to me—
alone.

3) Detail: Painted Faces

Poems come alive through details. Tell the students to imagine climbing inside of a flower. Ask, "What tiny details exist there? What does it smell like?" When they describe people, they need to get down to the wrinkles in their faces. They need to record their actions, little daily habits that are unique to them. The reader gets to know people this way—the way they drink their coffee, how they shuffle their feet, the colors in their eyes. Poets can paint portraits of people this way. Then ask a volunteer to read the first model poem.

"History," by Gary Soto

Grandma lit the stove.
Morning sunlight
Lengthened in spears
Across the linoleum floor.
Wrapped in a shawl,
Her eyes small
With sleep,
She sliced papas,
Pounded chiles
With a stone
Brought from Guadalajara.

                          After
Grandpa left for work,
She hosed down
The walk her sons paved
And in the shade
Of a chinaberry,
Unearthed her
Secret cigar box
Of bright coins
And bills, counted them
In English,
Then in Spanish,
And buried them elsewhere.
Later, back
From the market,
Where no one saw her,
She pulled out
Pepper and beet, spines
Of asparagus
From her blouse,
Tiny chocolates
From under a paisley bandana,
And smiled.

That was the '50s
And Grandma in her '50s,
A face streaked
From cutting grapes
And boxing plums.
I remember her insides
Were washed of tapeworm,
Her arms swelled into knobs
Of small growths—
Her second son

Dropped from a ladder
And was dust.
And yet I do not know
The sorrows
That sent her praying
In the dark of a closet,
The tear that fell
At night
When she touched
Loose skin
Of belly and breasts.
I do not know why
Her face shines
Or what goes beyond this shine,
Only the stories
That pulled her
From Taxco to San Joaquin,
Delano to Westside,
The places
In which we all begin.

Here the poet captures the grandma by telling the reader what she looks like: "Her eyes small/With sleep" and "A face streaked/From cutting grapes/And boxing plums." This also lets the reader know she's had a hard life. He also describes how she buries money in the yard, digs it up, and then counts it in both English and Spanish to be sure it's all still there.

Read the next model poem, which describes a father's daughter. The poet zeroes in on the expression on her face, "A solemnity so elegant/It must seem to some/The very definition of love." The point of view is from a protective father.

"Portrait," by David St. John

There is in his daughter's gaze
A solemnity so elegant
It must seem to some
The very definition of love

Though her profile guards
Any true window to emotion
Any genuine reflection of
Her understanding of her father's

Objective protective despair
As her beauty is shielded
By white & her lips in their easy
Parting draw back

From any kiss now
She is watching in the distance
Of the chapel a whole narrative
Beginning to assemble

One which finds the breath
Of the huge organ an unholy
Accompaniment its
Bellows moaning heavily over

What just a moment ago
The virginal & clear morning
Had promised to unveil forever
Yet which (now) the white day

Seems so certain to withhold

Now it's time to write. Ask the students to think of a person in their lives, a friend or relative, who has had a strong impact on them. It could be positive or negative. They can write the poem as an observer, like the speakers in two poems just read, or they can be in the poem interacting with the person.

The important thing is to describe the person with rich details that are unique to that person, in order to differentiate him or her from others. Readers want to know something intimate about that person in the end, something that makes her or him come alive. Also encourage them to take passages from their journals and incorporate them into their poems, if appropriate.

Here's an excerpt from a student poem that describes a security guard at the prison:

from "The Sergeant," by Arnie

His stripes scowl at me through the glass,
the uniform with the buckwheat haircut
beer belly flaunting my have-nots
authority taunting and threatening
profanity and disrespect flowing effortlessly
between the cattle rustler's moustache.

4) Emotion: Love Poems

Tell the students that when they express emotions in poems, they want readers to be able to step into the poem and make the experience theirs. They do not want their poem to deteriorate into vague conceptual ideas. Sensuality is also important. Discuss how when they write an erotic poem, they don't need to name body parts. They can describe what their lover smells like, for example, and the reader can imagine the rest.

Specifically ask them to write love poems. This will be a challenge for some hard-core inmates; however, if they get rid of the idea that love poems are all mushy and girly, then they can express what's inside of them and not feel vulnerable. Their poems can be about someone real or imaginary. They can be about someone real whom they fantasize about. It doesn't have to be the truth.

The first model poem is by Etheridge Knight, who grew up in the South, dropped out of high school and spent eight years in prison for a robbery conviction in the 1960s. That's when he started writing poetry, and one year before his release, Broadside Press published his first book, *Poems from Prison*. This poem is about a family visit while incarcerated. Ask a volunteer to read it.

"Upon Your Leaving," by Etheridge Knight
(for Sonia)
Night
and in the warm blackness
your woman smell filled the room
and our rivers flowed together, became one
my love's patterns. our sweat/drenched bellies
made flat cracks as we kissed
like sea waves lapping against the shore
rocks rising and rolling and sliding back.

And
your sighs softly calling my name
became love songs child/woman songs
as old as a thousand years new as the few
smiles you released like sacred doves. and I
fell asleep, ashamed of my glow, of my halo, and
ignoring them who waited below
to take you away when the sun rose. . . .

Day
and the sunlight playing in the green leaves
above us fell across your face traced the tears
in your eyes and love patterns in the wet grass.
and as they waited inside in triumphant patience
to take you away I begged you to stay.
"but, etheridge," you said, "i don't know what to do."
and the love patterns shifted and shimmered in your eyes.

And
after they had taken you and gone, the day
turned stark white. bleak. barren like
the nordic landscape. I turned and entered
into the empty house and fell on the floor.

laughing. trying to fill the spaces your love had left.
knowing that we would not remain apart long.
our rivers had flowed together.
we are one.
and are strong.

This next poem is very sensual, as Galway Kinnell uses his imagination to create erotic love imagery.

"Rapture," by Galway Kinnell

I can feel she has gotten out of bed.
That means it is seven A.M.
I have been lying with eyes shut,
thinking, or possibly dreaming,
of how she might look if, at breakfast,
I spoke about the hidden place in her
which, to me, is like a soprano's tremolo,
and right then, over toast and bramble jelly,
if such things are possible, she came.
I imagine she would show it while trying to conceal it.
I imagine her hair would fall about her face
and she would become apparently downcast,
as she does at a concert when she is moved.
The hypnopompic play passes, and I open my eyes
and there she is, next to the bed,
bending to a low drawer, picking over
various small smooth black, white,
and pink items of underwear. She bends
so low her back runs parallel to the earth,
but there is no sway in it, there is little burden, the day has hardly begun.
The two mounds of muscles for walking, leaping, lovemaking,
lift toward the east—what can I say?
Simile is useless; there is nothing like them on earth.
Her breasts fall full; the nipples
are deep pink in the glare shining up through the iron bars
of the gate under the earth where those who could not love
press, wanting to be born again.
I reach out and take her wrist
and she falls back into bed and at once starts unbuttoning my pajamas.
Later, when I open my eyes, there she is again,
rummaging in the same low drawer.
The clock shows eight. Hmmm.
With huge, silent effort of great,
mounded muscles the earth has been turning.

She takes a piece of silken cloth
from the drawer and stands up. Under the falls
of hair her face has become quiet and downcast,
as if she will be, all day among strangers,
looking down inside herself at our rapture.

Now it's time to write a love poem for or about someone. It can be a high school crush, first love, a girlfriend, wife, a friend, or a family member. It does not have to be romantic love, but it can be. It can also be about a love lost or unrequited love. Tell the students to say something to or about that person—directly or indirectly—that they've always wanted to say, but never could or would before.

The idea here is to express a strong emotion. Tell them not to feel bound by the topic; they can use their own ideas and branch out, if they want. The goal is also to take a risk and say something difficult in poetry form. They can feel free to embellish situations, too. Fantasy is good, and it's absolutely allowed.

Here's a love poem by a student:

"Shelley," by Chino

A rose fighting for existence among the thorns
Your armor is the kindness long forgotten

In my heart I hear your laughter could I join
And I would see children frolicking around a maypole

Time so little to share as your eyes sparkle
Hearing words which will not be denied

I place my hand in yours no longer do I hold
The sword of destruction but a pen of peace

Moonlit nights I will walk in memory of you
Until sunrise brings the image of your smile.

Appendix
Additional Exercise Ideas

- Write about feeling left out or hurt and turn it into pride.
- Write affirmations. Repeat "I am. . . ."
- Think about insects. How do you relate to these tiny creatures?
- Think about the food that you eat in your culture or your family. Who cooks it? What does it taste like? What's your favorite meal?
- Make something bigger. Imagine you could sleep on a leaf of grass or fly on a bumblebee.
- Write a list of questions with strange, imaginative answers.
- Write a tribute to an animal that you normally find disgusting, like an opossum.
- Write about being lost in the world.
- Imagine colors attached to sad, mad, or scary memories. Use colors to write about those memories.
- Take a trip on a time machine and go back to some place in the past. What happens there?
- Write in the persona of your worst enemy, and write from her or his point of view.
- Personify a poem. Give it a life. Pretend that it follows you around, sleeps with you, enters your dreams, knows what you like to eat or wear, and so forth.
- Give directions to your house, not in a traditional, boring way, but rather in a creative, imaginative way.
- Write a poem on conscience. Take a stand and either expose an injustice or describe something you don't like that's happening in the world.
- Write about hurt animals, victims of either our highways or pollution or natural phenomena.

- Find the light in your life and see how it's connected to something outside in the universe. How can it guide you or give you hope?
- Write about finding peace within.
- Write a narrative poem, a poem that tells a story about someone you know.
- Go inside of yourself and find a safe place to be, a place of retreat and comfort, a magical place that's only yours.

Permissions

Yehuda Amichai, "I Passed a House," translated by Glenda Abramson and Tutor Parfitt. Copyright © 1988 by Yehuda Amichai. Used with permission of Hana Amichai, Executor of Yehuda Amichai's Estate.
Jimmy Santiago Baca, "I Am Offering This Poem" and "Like an Animal" from IMMIGRANTS IN OUR OWN LAND, copyright © 1979 by Jimmy Santiago Baca. Reprinted by permission of New Directions Publishing Corp.
Michelle Bitting, "and in that moment I was happy" and "In Praise of My Brother, the Painter" from *Notes to the Beloved* (Sacramento Poetry Center Press). Copyright © 2011 by Michelle Bitting. Used by permission of the author.
Richard Blanco, "Islamorada" from *City of a Hundred Fires*, copyright © 1998 by Richard Blanco. Reprinted by permission of the University of Pittsburgh Press.
Richard Blanco, "Place of Mind" from *Looking for The Gulf Motel*, copyright © 2012 by Richard Blanco. Reprinted by permission of the University of Pittsburgh Press.
Robert Bly, "The Clear Air of October" from *Silence in the Snowy Fields*, Wesleyan University Press, Middletown, CT, copyright © 1962 by Robert Bly. Used with permission of the author.
California Poets in the Schools (CPITS) student poems that have appeared in their anthologies: "Woman," by Addy Reyes, "What Can I Do?" by LaQuinta Clark, "Migrating Birds," by Talia Savren, "Mamita," by Gaby Ramirez, "I Love You Brother," by Vincent Valentine, "Grace of a Falling Angel," by Jerome Woody, "First Kiss," by Mabel Robles, "Evan," by Andy Renshaw, and "Depression" by Courtney Adams. California Poets in the Schools grants permission to use these student poems. This book was made possible in part by the student poems that are a result of the CPITS program, and the book is produced in part to promote the CPITS mission.
Lucille Clifton, "flowers" from *The Collected Poems of Lucille Clifton*. Copyright © 1987 by Lucille Clifton. Reprinted with the permission of The Permissions Company, Inc. on behalf of BOA Editions, Ltd., www.boaeditions.org.

Lucille Clifton, "homage to my hips." Copyright © 1980 by Lucille Clifton. Now appears in *The Collected Poems of Lucille Clifton 1965–2010*, published by BOA Editions. Reprinted by permission of Curtis Brown, Ltd.

Molly Fisk, "Explanation" from *Listening to Winter*. Copyright © 2000 by Molly Fisk. Used by permission of the author. Poet, radio commentator, and life coach Molly Fisk lives in the Sierra Nevada foothills of California. "Explanation" is from her first collection, *Listening to Winter*, #4 in the California Poetry Series. She taught with CPITS in the 1990s and currently runs on-line writing classes at poetrybootcamp.com.

Carolyn Forché, "The Morning Baking" and "Blue Mesa" from GATHERING THE TRIBES. Copyright © 1976 by Carolyn Forché. Used by permission from Yale University Press.

Louise Gluck, "Gretel in Darkness" from THE FIRST FOUR BOOKS OF POEMS. Copyright © 1968, 1971, 1972, 1973, 1974, 1975, 1976, 1977, 1978, 1979, 1980, 1985, 1995 by Louise Gluck. Reprinted by permission of HarperCollins Publishers.

Judy Grahn, "VII. Vera, from my childhood," "The Common Woman Poems" from *love belongs to those who do the feeling*. Copyright © 2008 by Judy Grahn. Used by permission of Red Hen Press.

Jack Grapes, "The Lost Things," from *The Naked Eye: New & Selected Poems: 1987–2012* (Bombshelter Press). Copyright © 2012 by Jack Grapes. Used by permission of the author.

Sam Hamill, "Midsummer" from *Gratitude*. Copyright © 1998 by Sam Hamill. Used by permission of the author.

Eloise Klein Healy, "Raining" from *Passing*. Copyright © 2002 by Eloise Klein Healy. Used by permission of Red Hen Press.

Joy Harjo, "Remember." Copyright © 1983 by Joy Harjo, from SHE HAD SOME HORSES. Used by permission of the author and W. W. Norton & Company, Inc.

Jane Hirshfield, "Green-Striped Melons," copyright © Jane Hirshfield, from *Come Thief* (NY: Knopf, 2011). Used by permission of Jane Hirshfield. All rights reserved.

Jane Hirshfield, "Surrounded by All the Falling" from *Of Gravity & Angels*. Copyright © 2011 by Jane Hirshfield. Reprinted with permission of Wesleyan University Press.

Garrett Hongo, "The Legend" from RIVER OF HEAVEN, copyright © 1988 by Garrett Hongo. Used by permission of Alfred A. Knopf, an imprint of the Knopf Doubleday Publishing Group, a division of Penguin Random House LLC. All rights reserved.

Marie Howe, "Sometimes the Moon Sat in the Well at Night," from THE KINGDOM OF ORDINARY TIME. Copyright © 2008 by Marie Howe. Used by permission of the author and W. W. Norton & Company, Inc.

Elijah Imlay, "War Dog" and "Bird Grieves for the Man They Killed" from *Monsoon Blues*. Copyright © 2011 by Elijah Imlay. Used with permission from the author and publisher, Tebot Bach.

Brigit Pegeen Kelly, "The Leaving" from TO THE PLACE OF TRUMPETS. Copyright © 1999 by Brigit Pegeen Kelly. Used by permission from Yale University Press.

Jane Kenyon, "Peonies at Dusk" from *Collected Poems*. Copyright © 2005 by the Estate of Jane Kenyon. Reprinted with the permission of The Permissions Company, Inc. on behalf of Graywolf Press, Minneapolis, Minnesota, www.graywolfpress.org.

Galway Kinnell, "Rapture" from IMPERFECT THIRST: Poems by Galway Kinnell. Copyright © 1994 by Galway Kinnell. Reprinted by permission of Houghton Mifflin Harcourt Publishing Company. All rights reserved.

Carolyn Kizer, "For Jan, in Bar Maria" from *Mermaids in the Basement: Poems for Women*. Copyright © 1984 by Carolyn Kizer. Reprinted with the permission of The Permissions Company, Inc. on behalf of Copper Canyon Press, www.coppercanyonpress.org.

Etheridge Knight, "Upon Your Leaving" and "A Poem for Myself (or Blues for a Mississippi Black Boy)" from *The Essential Etheridge Knight*, copyright © 1986 by Etheridge Knight. Reprinted by permission of the University of Pittsburgh Press.

Dorianne Laux, "Cher," from THE BOOK OF MEN. Copyright © 2011 by Dorianne Laux. Used by permission of W. W. Norton & Company, Inc.

Dorianne Laux, "Singing Back the World" from *What We Carry*. Copyright © 1994 by Dorianne Laux. Reprinted with the permission of The Permissions Company, Inc. on behalf of BOA Editions, Ltd., www.boaeditions.org.

Li-Young Lee, "I Ask My Mother to Sing" and "The Gift" from *Rose*. Copyright © 1986 by Li-Young Lee. Reprinted with the permission of The Permissions Company, Inc. on behalf of BOA Editions, Ltd., www.boaeditions.org.

Denise Levertov, "A Woman Alone" from LIFE IN THE FOREST, copyright © 1978 by Denise Levertov. Reprinted by permission of New Directions Publishing Corp.

Philip Levine, "The Mercy" from THE MERCY: POEMS, copyright © 1999 by Philip Levine. Used by permission of Alfred A. Knopf, an imprint of the Knopf Doubleday Publishing Group, a division of Penguin Random House LLC. All rights reserved.

Peter Levitt, "This Shore" from *Bright Root, Dark Root*, Broken Moon Press. Copyright © 1991 by Peter Levitt. Used with permission from author.

Perie Longo, "Fishing with my Father" and "My Everything." Copyright © 2014 by Perie Longo. Reprinted from *Baggage Claim*, published by WordTech Editions, Cincinnati, OH, 2014.

Audre Lorde, "Black Mother Woman." Copyright © 1973 by Audre Lorde, from THE COLLECTED POEMS OF AUDRE LORDE. Used by permission of the author and W. W. Norton & Company, Inc.

Audre Lorde, "Coping," from THE BLACK UNICORN. Copyright © 1978 by Audre Lorde. Used by permission of W. W. Norton & Company, Inc.

Glenna Luschei, "The New House" from *Salt Lick*, copyright © 2009 by Glenna Luschei. Used with permission from author.

W. S. Merwin, "Dusk in Winter" from THE SECOND FOUR BOOKS OF POEMS. Copyright © 1960, 1961, 1962, 1963, 1964, 1965, 1966, 1967, 1968, 1969, 1970, 1971, 1972, 1973, 1993 by W. S. Merwin, used by permission of The Wylie Agency LLC.

Pablo Neruda, "The Queen" and "Wind on the Island" from THE CAPTAIN'S VERSES, copyright © 1972 by Pablo Neruda and Donald D. Walsh. Reprinted by permission of New Directions Publishing Corp.

Naomi Shihab Nye, "Kindness" from *Words Under the Words: Selected Poems*, copyright © 1995 by Naomi Shihab Nye. Used by permission of the author, Naomi Shihab Nye, 2015.

Sharon Olds, "I Go Back to May 1937" from THE GOLD CELL, copyright © 1987 by Sharon Olds. Used by permission of Alfred A. Knopf, an imprint of the Knopf Doubleday Publishing Group, a division of Penguin Random House LLC. All rights reserved.

Mary Oliver, "The Rapture" from WEST WIND: Poems and Prose Poems. Copyright © 1997 by Mary Oliver. Reprinted by permission of Houghton Mifflin Harcourt Publishing Company. All rights reserved.

Alicia Susan Ostriker, "The Wind That Blows Through Me" from *The Old Woman, the Tulip, and the Dog*, copyright © 2013 by Alicia Susan Ostriker. Reprinted by permission of the University of Pittsburgh Press.

Oxnard College students. The following students have granted permission to use their poems: "Moving Day" and "Love Like" by Fiona Cox, "To My Book" by Krista Roque, "Pity the American Dandelion" by Alina Rutschley, and "Prince William" by Vanessa Johnson.

Marge Piercy, "The woman in the ordinary," from CIRCLES ON THE WATER, copyright © 1982 by Middlemarsh, Inc. Used by permission of Alfred A. Knopf, an imprint of the Knopf Doubleday Publishing Group, a division of Penguin Random House LLC. All rights reserved.

Sylvia Plath, all lines from "Mirror" from CROSSING THE WATER. Copyright © 1963 by Ted Hughes. Originally appeared in *The New Yorker*. Reprinted by permission of HarperCollins Publishers.

Adrienne Rich, Poem IX of "Twenty-One Love Poems," from THE DREAM OF A COMMON LANGUAGE: Poems 1974–1977. Copyright © 1978 by W. W. Norton & Company, Inc. Used by permission of W. W. Norton & Company, Inc.

Adrienne Rich, "The Stranger," from DIVING INTO THE WRECK: Poems 1971–1972. Copyright © 1973 by W. W. Norton & Company, Inc. Used by permission of W. W. Norton & Company, Inc.

Jalal ad-Din Rumi, "Come to the orchard in spring," translated by Coleman Barks, copyright © by Coleman Barks. Used by permission of Coleman Barks.

Shelley Savren, "First Gig" from *Where Animals Move Like Planets* (California Poets in the Schools anthology). Copyright © 2015 by Shelley Savren.

Shelley Savren, "Pricilla's Journal," "She Wanted Vegas," "The Boy Who Eats Worms," "The Kids' Shelter and the Senior Center," "Leaping onto a Page," "Finding the Women's Center," and "Chino" from *The Wild Shine of Oranges* (Tebot Bach Press). Copyright © 2013 by Shelley Savren. Used by permission of the author.

Shelley Savren, "Welcome This Graduation Day" from *My Mouth the Galaxy* (California Poets in the Schools anthology). Copyright © 2015 by Shelley Savren. Used by permission of the author.

Anne Sexton, "The Breast" from LOVE POEMS. Copyright © 1967, 1968, 1969 by Anne Sexton. Reprinted by permission of Houghton Mifflin Harcourt Publishing Company. All rights reserved.

Anne Sexton, "Rapunzel" from TRANSFORMATIONS. Copyright © 1971 by Anne Sexton, renewed 1999 by Linda G. Sexton. Reprinted by permission of Houghton Mifflin Harcourt Publishing Company. All rights reserved.

Gary Soto, "History" from *New and Selected Poems*. Copyright © 1995 by Gary Soto. Used with permission of Chronicle Books LLC, San Francisco. Visit ChronicleBooks.com.

Elizabeth Spires, "Easter Sunday, 1955," from WORLDLING. Copyright © 1995 by Elizabeth Spires. Used by permission of the author and W. W. Norton & Company, Inc.

David St. John, "Iris" from *Study for the World's Body: New and Selected Poems*. Copyright © 1994 by David St. John. Used with permission of author.

David St. John, "Portrait" from *The Red Leaves of Night*. Copyright © 1999 by David St. John. Used with permission of the author.

Gerald Stern, "Washington Square," from THIS TIME: NEW AND SELECTED POEMS. Copyright © 1998 by Gerald Stern. Used by permission of the author and W. W. Norton & Company, Inc.

Wallace Stevens, "Thirteen Ways of Looking at a Blackbird," from THE COLLECTED POEMS OF WALLACE STEVENS, copyright © 1954 by Wallace Stevens and copyright renewed 1982 by Holly Stevens. Used by permission of Alfred A. Knopf, an imprint of the Knopf Doubleday Publishing Group, a division of Penguin Random House LLC. All rights reserved.

May Swenson, "Analysis of Baseball" from *New and Selected Things Taking Place*. Copyright © 1978 by May Swenson. Used with permission of The Literary Estate of May Swenson. All rights reserved.

Amy Uyematsu, "The Painter" from *The Yellow Door*. Copyright © 2015 by Amy Uyematsu. Used by permission of Red Hen Press.

Patrice Vecchione, "The Sadness I Live For" and "At the Gate to Desolation Wilderness" from *Territory of Wind*, copyright © 1998 by Patrice Vecchione. Used by permission of the author. In addition to *Territory of Wind*, her other collection of poetry is *The Knot Untied*. Patrice's newest nonfiction book is *Step into Nature: Nurturing Imagination and Spirit in Everyday Life* (Simon & Schuster/Beyond Words/Atria Books). patricevecchione.com.

Bruce Weigl, "Snowy Egret" from *Song of Napalm* (Grove/Atlantic), copyright © 1988 by Bruce Weigl. Used by permission of the author.

Bruce Weigl, "I Almost Didn't See" from *Abundance of Nothing* (Triquarterly Books), copyright © 2012 by Bruce Weigl. Used by permission of the author.

Susan G. Wooldridge, "My Shadow" from *poemcrazy: freeing your life with words*, copyright © 1996 by Susan G. Wooldridge. Used by permission of the author.

James Wright, "A Blessing" from *Above the River*. Copyright © 1990 by James Wright. Reprinted with permission of Wesleyan University Press.

Resources

Academy of American Poets: www.poets.org
Association of Writers & Writing Programs: www.awpwriter.org
California Poets in the Schools: www.cpits.org
Poetry Foundation: www.poetryfoundation.org
Poetry Out Loud: www.poetryoutloud.org
Poets & Writers: www.pw.org
Teachers & Writers Collaborative: www.twc.org

Index

alliteration, 10–11, 73, 81, 83, 84, 89
Amichai, Yehuda (trans. Glenda Abramson and Tudor Parfitt): "I Passed a House," 76–77
"Analysis of Baseball" (May Swenson), 81–82
"and in that moment I was happy" (Michelle Bitting), 140–141
"At the Gateway to Desolation Wilderness" (Patrice Vecchione), 153–154

Baca, Jimmy Santiago: "I Am Offering This Poem," 150; "Like an Animal," 78
"Bird Grieves for the Man They Killed" (Elijah Imlay), 36–37
Bitting, Michelle: "and in that moment I was happy," 140–141; "In Praise of My Brother, the Painter," 116
"Black Mother Woman" (Audre Lorde), 142
Blake, William: "The Tyger," 63
Blanco, Richard: "Islamorada," 59; "Place of Mind," 73
"A Blessing" (James Wright), 152–153

"Blue Mesa" (Carolyn Forché), 110
Bly, Robert: "The Clear Air of October," 128
"The Boy Who Eats Worms" (Shelley Savren), 68–69
"The Breast" (Anne Sexton), 137
Byron, (Lord) George Gordon: "She Walks in Beauty," 65

"Cher" (Dorianne Laux), 66
"Chino" (Shelley Savren), 145–146
"The Clear Air of October" (Robert Bly), 128
Clifton, Lucille: "flowers," 123; "homage to my hips," 137
color, 8, 9, 97, 98, 123, 153, 163
"Come to the orchard in spring. . ." (Jalal ad-Din Rumi, trans. Coleman Barks), 60
"Coping" (Audre Lorde), 22
critiquing, 11, 17, 90, 91, 92

details, 8, 50, 51, 52, 53, 60, 62, 66, 90, 105, 151, 155
"Dusk in Winter" (W. S. Merwin), 126

"Easter Sunday, 1955" (Elizabeth Spires), 50–51
"Explanation" (Molly Fisk), 46–47

feelings (emotions), 9, 23, 35, 52, 62, 74, 98, 115, 126, 139, 158
"Finding the Women's Center" (Shelley Savren), 131
"First Gig" (Shelley Savren), 15–16
"Fishing with my Father" (Perie Longo), 33–34
Fisk, Molly:
   "Explanation," 46–47
five senses (perception), 8, 21, 33, 60, 98, 109, 123, 136
"flowers" (Lucille Clifton), 123
Forché, Carolyn:
   "Blue Mesa," 110;
   "The Morning Baking," 27–28
"For Jan, in Bar Maria" (Carolyn Kizer), 24–25
form, 11, 88, 133

"The Gift" (Li-Young Lee), 99
Glück, Louise:
   "Gretel in Darkness," 31–32
Grahn, Judy:
   "VII. Vera, from my childhood," 135
Grapes, Jack:
   "The Lost Things," 74–76
"Green-Striped Melons" (Jane Hirshfield), 128
"Gretel in Darkness" (Louise Glück), 31–32

Hamill, Sam:
   "Midsummer," 148–149
Harjo, Joy:
   "Remember," 93–94
Healy, Eloise Klein:
   "Raining," 21–22
Hirshfield, Jane:
   "Green-Striped Melons," 128;
   "Surrounded by All the Falling," 19
"History" (Gary Soto), 156–157
"homage to my hips" (Lucille Clifton), 137
Hongo, Garrett:
   from "The Legend," 95
Howe, Marie:

from "Sometimes the Moon Sat in the Well at Night," 124

"I Almost Didn't See" (Bruce Weigl), 63–64
"I Am Offering This Poem" (Jimmy Santiago Baca), 150
"I Ask My Mother to Sing" (Li-Young Lee), 58
"I Go Back to May 1937" (Sharon Olds), 97
imagery, 9, 26, 38, 48, 65, 78, 79, 89, 95, 127, 141, 142, 152
imagination, 7, 8, 9, 18, 29, 46, 57, 65, 71, 93, 94, 106, 122, 134, 148
Imlay, Elijah:
   "Bird Grieves for the Man They Killed," 36–37;
   "War Dog," 60–61
"In Praise of My Brother, the Painter" (Michelle Bitting), 116
"I Passed a House" (Yehuda Amichai, trans. Glenda Abramson and Tudor Parfitt), 76–77
"Iris" (David St. John), 39–40
"Islamorada" (Richard Blanco), 59

Kelly, Brigit Pegeen:
   "The Leaving," 78–79
Kenyon, Jane:
   "Peonies at Dusk," 101
"The Kids' Shelter and the Senior Center" (Shelley Savren), 103
"Kindness" (Naomi Shihab Nye), 40–41
Kinnell, Galway:
   "Rapture," 160–161
Kizer, Carolyn:
   "For Jan, in Bar Maria," 24–25
Knight, Etheridge:
   "A Poem for Myself (or Blues for a Mississippi Black Boy)," 83;
   "Upon Your Leaving," 159–160
Kunitz, Stanley:
   "The Portrait," 51–52

Laux, Dorianne:

from "Cher," 66;
"Singing Back the World," 23–24
"Leaping onto a Page" (Shelley
    Savren), 119–120
"The Leaving" (Brigit Pegeen Kelly),
    78
Lee, Li-Young:
    "The Gift," 99;
    "I Ask My Mother to Sing," 58
"The Legend" (Garrett Hongo), 95
Levertov, Denise:
    "A Woman Alone," 112–113
Levine, Philip:
    "The Mercy," 107
Levitt, Peter:
    "This Shore," 124–125
"Like an Animal" (Jimmy Santiago
    Baca), 78
Longo, Perie:
    "Fishing with my Father," 33–34;
    "My Everything," 108
Lorde, Audre:
    "Black Mother Woman," 142;
    "Coping," 22
"The Lost Things" (Jack Grapes),
    74–76
Luschei, Glenna:
    "The New House," 53

"The Mercy" (Philip Levine), 107
Merwin, W. S.:
    "Dusk in Winter," 126
metaphor, 10, 65, 89, 111, 116, 141,
    142, 152
"Midsummer" (Sam Hamill), 148–149
"Mirror" (Sylvia Plath), 113
"The Morning Baking" (Carolyn
    Forché), 27–28
"My Everything" (Perie Longo), 108
"My Shadow" (Susan Wooldridge),
    48–49

Neruda, Pablo (trans. Donald D. Walsh):
    "The Queen," 20;
    "Wind on the Island," 115–116
"The New House" (Glenna Luschei), 53

"IX" (Adrienne Rich), 110
Nye, Naomi Shihab:
    "Kindness," 40–41

Olds, Sharon:
    "I Go Back to May 1937," 97
Oliver, Mary:
    "The Rapture," 142–143
Ostriker, Alicia:
    "The Wind That Blows Through
    Me," 126

"The Painter" (Amy Uyematsu), 72
"Peonies at Dusk" (Jane Kenyon), 101
persona, 10, 46, 78, 79, 89, 114, 163
personification, 10, 41, 48, 89, 101, 108,
    110, 114, 126
Piercy, Marge:
    "The woman in the ordinary,"
    134–135
"Place of Mind" (Richard Blanco), 73
Plath, Sylvia:
    "Mirror," 113
"A Poem for Myself (or Blues for
    a Mississippi Black Boy)"
    (Etheridge Knight), 83
"the poet's eye. . ." (William
    Shakespeare), vii
"Portrait" (David St. John), 157
"The Portrait" (Stanley Kunitz), 51
"Priscilla's Journal" (Shelley Savren),
    43–44

"The Queen" (Pablo Neruda, trans.
    Donald D. Walsh), 20

"Raining" (Eloise Klein Healy), 21–22
"Rapture" (Galway Kinnell), 160–161
"The Rapture" (Mary Oliver), 142–143
"Rapunzel" (Anne Sexton), 29–31
"Remember" (Joy Harjo), 93–94
revision, 12, 17, 88, 92
rhythm, 4, 10, 11, 51, 81, 83, 89
Rich, Adrienne:
    "IX," 110;
    "The Stranger," 139–140

Rumi, Jalal ad-Din (trans. Coleman Barks):
"Come to the orchard in spring...," 60

"The Sadness I Live For" (Patrice Vecchione), 26–27
Savren, Shelley:
"The Boy Who Eats Worms," 68–69;
"Chino," 145–146;
"Finding the Women's Center," 131;
"First Gig," 15–16;
"The Kids' Shelter and the Senior Center," 103;
"Leaping onto a Page," 119–120;
"Priscilla's Journal," 43–44;
"She Wanted Vegas," 55;
"Welcome This Graduation Day," 85–86
"VII. Vera, from my childhood" (Judy Grahn), 135
Sexton, Anne:
"The Breast," 137;
from "Rapunzel," 29–30
Shakespeare, William:
"The poet's eye...," vii
"She Walks in Beauty" (George Gordon, Lord Byron), 65
"She Wanted Vegas" (Shelley Savren), 55
simile, 10, 31, 41, 62, 64, 65, 66, 77, 79, 89, 101, 121, 127, 128, 129, 141, 143, 152, 153, 154
"Singing Back the World" (Dorianne Laux), 23–24
"Snowy Egret" (Bruce Weigl), 35–36
"Sometimes the Moon Sat in the Well at Night" (Marie Howe), 124
Soto, Gary:
"History," 156–157
Spires, Elizabeth:
"Easter Sunday, 1955," 50–51
Stern, Gerald:
from "Washington Square," 47
Stevens, Wallace:
from "Thirteen Ways of Looking at a Blackbird," 122

St. John, David:
"Iris," 39–40;
"Portrait," 157
"The Stranger" (Adrienne Rich), 139–140
"Surrounded by All the Falling" (Jane Hirshfield), 19
Swenson, May:
"Analysis of Baseball," 81–82

"Thirteen Ways of Looking at a Blackbird" (Wallace Stevens), 122
"This Shore" (Peter Levitt), 124–125
"The Tyger" (William Blake), 63

Uyematsu, Amy:
"The Painter," 72
"Upon Your Leaving" (Etheridge Knight), 159–160

Vecchione, Patrice:
"At the Gateway to Desolation Wilderness," 153–154;
"The Sadness I Live For," 26–27

"War Dog" (Elijah Imlay), 60–61
"Washington Square" (Gerald Stern), 47
Weigl, Bruce:
"I Almost Didn't See," 63–64;
"Snowy Egret," 35–36
"Welcome This Graduation Day" (Shelley Savren), 85–86
"Wind on the Island" (Pablo Neruda, trans. Donald D. Walsh), 115–116
"The Wind That Blows Through Me" (Alicia Ostriker), 126
Wooldridge, Susan:
"My Shadow," 48–49
"A Woman Alone" (Denise Levertov), 112–113
"the woman in the ordinary" (Marge Piercy), 134–135
Wright, James:
"A Blessing," 152–153

About the Author

Since January 1976, **Shelley Savren** has taught poetry-writing workshops to over twenty-five thousand people, including pre-K through college students, homeless children, abused and neglected youths, adolescents with mental health issues, and developmentally disabled adults. She has taught in hundreds of classrooms, including a maximum-security men's prison, juvenile halls, art museums, a senior center, and women's centers. Ms. Savren's workshops have been featured in several newspapers, such as the *Los Angeles Times*, the *Ventura County Star*, and the *San Diego Union-Tribune*, which has written, "By helping people know the world about them, perceive it with all of their senses, Shelley Savren helps them stretch their imaginations."

Ms. Savren is the author of two poetry collections, *The Common Fire* and *The Wild Shine of Oranges*. Her poetry has been published widely in literary magazines, including *Prairie Schooner, Solo, Rattle, Main Street Rag, Solstice: A Magazine of Diverse Voices*, and *Serving House Journal*, and she has read at universities, libraries, and coffeehouses across the United States.

Ms. Savren's awards include the John David Johnson Memorial Poetry Award, Rainer Maria Rilke International Poetry Competition, Cleveland State University Poetry Center Prize (finalist for *The Common Fire*), and University of Arkansas Press Poetry Series Prize (semifinalist for *The Wild Shine of Oranges*). She has received nine California Arts Council Artist-in-Residence grants, three NEA regional grants, five artist fellowships from the City of Ventura, and a nomination for a Pushcart Prize.

Ms. Savren has conducted many in-service workshops for teachers and trained dozens of poets to conduct poetry-writing workshops. She is a fellow of the South Coast Writing Project, a local chapter of the National Writing Project, and holds a BA from Ohio State University, an MA from Central Michigan University, and an MFA from Antioch University, Los Angeles. She is a professor emeritus of English and creative writing at Oxnard College, Oxnard, California. Visit her website at www.shelleysavren.com.

www.ingramcontent.com/pod-product-compliance
Lightning Source LLC
Chambersburg PA
CBHW030112010526
44116CB00005B/209